JESUS CHRIST Son of the Living God
Understanding the revelation that builds the ekklesia

PUBLISHED BY
KINGDOM WORD PUBLICATIONS
ALBION, MICHIGAN 49224
Printed in the U.S,A

JESUS CHRIST Son of the Living God
Understanding the revelation that builds the ekklesia

ISBN 978-0-9988952-6-0 Paperback
ISBN 978-0-9988952-7-7 ebook

Library of Congress Control Number: 2020946831

All references to satan and the devil are not capitalized in this book, even when it is literarily proper to do so.

The Greek word 'ekklesia' has been inserted in most scriptural references where the word 'church' was used.

KINGDOM WORD PUBLICATIONS is the publishing division of THE EKKLESIA CENTER. The mission of Kingdom Word Publications is to produce and distribute quality books, videos, and training materials to strengthen and empower believers. All material is provided to increase a greater understanding of the Lord's ekklesia. We encourage believers to gather from house to house according to the values and structure of first century Christianity.

For more information, visit our website www.TheEkklesiaCenter.org

TABLE OF CONTENTS

Acknowledgments   iv

Introduction   vii

1 | CAESAREA PHILIPPI   1

2 | ANOTHER JESUS   13

3 | HE KNOWS MY NAME   29

4 | REVEALING OUR MOTIVES   39

5 | EXPLORING HIS DEITY: BIRTH, LIFE AND DEATH   53

6 | THE BODILY RESURRECTION   67

7 | Culture, Ideology and Race   83

8 | RELIGION OR REVELATION   99

9 | BECOMING POSITIONED FOR REVELATION   113

10 | THE POWER IN THE NAME OF JESUS   125

11 | WHAT WILL IT TAKE FOR YOU   135

12 | JESUS CHRIST SON OF THE LIVING GOD   149

Acknowledgements

Although I should not be, I am amazed when I see what the Lord has show me in private times of prayer, come to life in those around me. I am eternally grateful to those who have stepped out and followed the message of the Lord's ekklesia that God has given me.

To Four Winds Christian Center, Real Life Ministries and New Life Ministries International, I am grateful for the trust you have given me. You represent three diverse gatherings of believers who have seen the Lord's ekklesia. Piece by piece you are helping to bring it to life in our region.

Dr. Leonard Robinson, your insight and teaching regarding the Kingdom of God is invaluable. Your contribution to this book regarding the culture of the Kingdom is profoundly appreciated. Thank you for adding to this work. (Read more about Dr. Robinson at the end of this book)

I write, but the editing work that Kat Wheeler puts into each of my books is priceless. Every word, every sentence, every paragraph, and every scripture reference is carefully reviewed. She is a tremendous asset to my ministry assignment.

As I write this, I have been in my office since about 5 a.m. It is now 4 p.m. It is the day after our 47th wedding anniversary. Yet, my wife Carolyn has allowed me to disappear in this space knowing that I need this time to complete this book. Every time I look at her I am reminded of how blessed I am to be married to her.

This book is about the Lordship of Jesus Christ. I could not write this book without personally having the revelation that He is the Christ, Son of the Living God. Over the approximately two years I have worked on this manuscript, the Holy Spirit often made sure that what I have written is supported by the fact that I personally have the revelation of Jesus Christ. It would be duplic-itous for me to write from theory rather than personal experience. I truly give thanks to my Living Lord for entrusting me with this assignment.

Finally, I thank you for reading this book. I pray that this will result in a greater revelation of Jesus Christ in your life.

Blessings!

Tim Kurtz

DEDICATED TO THE ARMY OF 'THE CALLED-OUT'

INTRODUCTION

Wednesday. February 13, 1974, I had reluctantly agreed to attend one night of a revival service at the request of Pastor Robert Brown. Grace Temple Church of God In Christ was a relatively new ministry at that time, but it was growing at a fast pace. The church building had been converted from a night club that ironically, I had performed in with my R & B group.

I entered the small building and took a seat as far back in the auditorium as I could find. I have joked that I was so far back that cars entering the parking lot had to drive around me to park. But there I was, sitting uncomfortably and listening to a sermon by the guest speaker, Pastor James Taylor. No, not the famous singer with the same name, but without question there was fire and rain that night. Pastor Taylor preached like fire and the power of God was raining down in the room. I cannot remember what his message was, but I can tell you something unexplainable was happening in me.

The time came for the traditional altar call. People were finding their way up front for prayer. And as if on cue, the ushers stood in front of the exit doors. They had effectively blocked my escape. Pastor Brown worked his way from the front towards where I was trying to hide. He pointed to me and beckoned me to come to the altar. My brains said, "Don't move", but my legs seem to go into autopilot and started carrying me to the altar. Before I could resist, I was literally leaping like a contestant who had just heard their name called on the Price Is Right.

I don't mean to trivialize the events of that night. Something marvelous was happening in me. Something I could not explain. After Pastors Taylor and Brown prayed over me, Pastor Brown asked me did I want to be saved. This was different from the religious tradition I grew up in. In times like these, I was used to the Pastor 'opening the doors of the church'. If I agreed, I would commit to joining that church, then receive the 'right hand of fellowship', and become a member. But Pastor Brown said nothing about joining the church, he only asked if I wanted to be saved. I did not contemplate my response. I just said, "Yes".

For the first time in my life, I repeated Romans 10:9. I opened my mouth and confessed the best I knew how, the Lord Jesus. I was saved. Looking back, I did not fully understand what I had done, but it was enough at that moment to literally change the trajectory of my life.

My abridged testimony is a necessary introduction to this book. The experience you had when you came to faith may differ, but generally the principle of confessing the Lord Jesus was similar. The confession we all made is significant to what I pray you will discover in each chapter of this book. Let's take a few moments to unpack Romans 10:9 as well as the two verses that follow.

That if thou shalt confess with thy mouth the Lord Jesus, and shalt believe in thine heart that God hath raised him from the dead, thou shalt be saved. For with the heart man believeth unto righteousness; and with the mouth confession is made unto salvation. For the scripture saith, Whosoever believeth on him shall not be ashamed. (Romans 10:9-11)

That wonderful Wednesday night I simply said that I 'confess the Lord Jesus'. In my mind, it was the equivalent of saying, "I believe in Jesus." Over the years I have found other bible translations that render this verse with more clarity. The confession that scripture says is to be made is that Jesus is Lord.[1] That confession is to be supported by the belief that God raised Jesus from the dead. To be honest, that latter part was easier for me to say but much harder to prove. The resurrection will be discussed in greater detail in this book.

What you believe regarding the resurrection is a critical component to your salvation (1Corinthians 15:13-17). The reality of the resurrection fuels your ability to function in the earth as an ambassador of the Kingdom of Heaven (2Corinthians 5:20). Everything, I repeat everything, you understand going forward rests on the eternal truth that Jesus Christ is declared to be the Living Son of the Living God with power. This declaration is according to the spirit of holiness by the resurrection of the dead (Romans 1:4).

---

[1] See The Amplified Bible, American Standard Version, The Revised Standard Version, The New Revised Standard Version, The Bible In Basic English, The New American Standard Version, and The World English Bible

Romans 10:10 makes it clear that what you believe in your heart, your inner most being, will set you in a place of right standing from heaven's view. It is then that your confession brings you into the realm of safety, healing, deliverance and unprecedented power. The promise that sums this up is that anyone who believes or confesses the Lordship of Jesus Christ at this level will never be ashamed. In other words, they can live confidently in the power of the risen Lord (Philippians 3:10).

Paul's instruction to the Romans can be traced back to the time when the eternal identity of Jesus Christ was declared by Peter. God had previously declared Jesus as His beloved Son (Matthew 3:17). John the Baptist declared Jesus to be the Lamb of God (John 1:29). However, it was on the coast of Caesarea Philippi that Peter said that Jesus is the Christ, Son of the Living God (Matthew 16:16).

Jesus made it clear that Peter's declaration was not the words of a mortal man. It was a revelation from God Himself. It is more than a religious affirmation encased in ritual and tradition. It is a deep inward knowing that impacts everything in your life. Yet, many believers have not come to grips with the magnitude of this revelation. This is what this book is about.

GET READY FOR REVELATION

This book will most likely be read by believers. It is not written to question anyone's salvation. The purpose is to bring believers into a greater revelation of the Son of God.

Jesus said that He would build His ekklesia with those who have the revelation that He is the Christ, Son of the Living God. Ironically, He later instructed His disciples not to tell anyone that He was Jesus the Christ (Matthew 16:16-20). Why, because only those who have a deep inner knowing of Jesus' identity as the Son of God will be empowered to carry out kingdom directives. I can tell you all day that Jesus is the Son of God, but your response to the world will expose if your knowledge of Jesus is cerebral or revelatory.

What do I mean by revelation? Revelation transitions a believer from just knowing *about* Jesus in a historical sense, to knowing Jesus as the living, ever present friend, partner and confidant in every matter of life (2Timothy 1:12). Revelation takes believers out of the realm of believing *in* Him into believing Him at all cost. Afterall, the devils believe and tremble (James 2:19). Believing Him is revelatory. It causes you to see the world around you from His view. Most importantly, this revelatory sight enables you to respond according to Kingdom directives.

> *I will give you the keys (authority) of the kingdom of heaven; and whatever you bind [forbid, declare to be improper and unlawful] on earth* [A]WILL HAVE [ALREADY] BEEN BOUND *in heaven, and whatever you loose [permit, declare lawful] on earth* [B]WILL HAVE [ALREADY] BEEN LOOSED *in heaven." (Matthew 16:19 Amplified Bible)*

The only way the ekklesia will have the authority and power to bind and loose, is by having the revelation of Jesus being the Christ, Son of the Living God. Sadly, the church generally only recognizes Jesus in context of their denominational distinctives. The church, as we know it, is changing. Economic, political and social pressures are exposing its true foundation. Unfortunately, racial, ideological, and doctrinal presuppositions have often been the rule within it. I stop short of saying many churches have followed doctrines of devils, but I will say that many churches have been built on humanistic belief systems that are no longer working (1Timothy 4:1-3).

We cannot claim that the problems we face today hinder us from walking in the true revelation of our Lord. The ekklesia grew in the first three centuries following Pentecost. They grew in spite of the resistance they encountered from the political, religious, social and economic pressures against them. It was not easy for the early believers to demonstrably live by the power of the resurrected Lord. Roland Allen, a twentieth century missionary to China wrote:

> We are sometimes apt to think that the social condition of those to whom St Paul preached may account for his success in establishing the [Church], and the answer comes with irresistible force that the majority of St Paul's converts were born and bred in an atmosphere certainly not better, and in some respects even worse, than that with which we have to deal today in India or China.

As I write this book, the world is reeling from the effects of the global corona virus pandemic. There is an acceleration of racial strife throughout the United States and the world. Social upheaval is on the rise at a dramatic rate. Political dysfunction and incompetence are being exposed in nearly every mainstream country. There are news reports claiming that Australia and southwestern United States are battling the worst wildfires they have faced in modern history. In addition, parts of both Australia and East Africa have what is described as locust invasions of biblical proportions.

Religious deception has cast a thick cloud over the minds of many. Yet, scripture has alerted us to times like these (Matthew 24:4-7; 1Timothy 4:1; 2Timothy 3:1-7). It requires a special people to navigate through this season.

See that you do not refuse Him who speaks. For if they did not escape who refused Him who spoke on earth, much more shall we not escape if we turn away from Him who speaks from heaven, whose voice then shook the earth; but now He has promised, saying, "Yet once more I shake not only the earth, but also heaven." Now this, "Yet once more," indicates the removal of those things that are being shaken, as of things that are made, that the things which cannot be shaken may remain. Therefore, since we are receiving a kingdom which cannot be shaken, let us have grace, by which we may serve God acceptably with reverence and godly fear. For our God is a consuming fire. (Hebrews 12:25-29)

I believe we are in a time of shaking. This shaking is not demonic. It is the voice that speaks from heaven that causes the shaking. It is the risen Lord who is speaking (Hebrews 1:1-2). The scripture clearly states that God said He would shake both earth and heaven. Shaking removes anything that can be shaken leaving only what is unshakeable. Shaking is an act necessary to align us with the unshakeable kingdom.

Both earth and heaven are being shaken. It is easy to see the effects of shaking in the earth, but how do we know that heaven is being shaken? First, be clear that the sovereign Kingdom of God is not being shaken (Daniel 7:14, 27). The heaven that is being shaken is the spiritual realms around the earth. It is the realm of principalities and powers in heavenly places who are vying for control over humanity (Ephesians 6:12). This manifests as a confusing and often contradictory array of ideologies, philosophies, the propagation of destructive lifestyles, and the devaluing of human life. The rise of racial conflicts, abortion, same sex marriage, false doctrines in the church system, political policies that codify injustice are just the tip of the iceberg of things being orchestrated by this lower level of heaven being shaken.

Recently, during a regional prayer session, one of the participants made a profound statement. She said, "Lord, we can trust You in the shaking!" Such a statement could only be made by a person whose eyes are on the Lord Jesus Christ. He is Lord over all principalities, thrones, powers and dominions (Ephesians 1:18-23; Colossians 2:10; 1Peter 3:21-22).

Throughout this book I will attempt to strip away the layers of religious, social, ideological, racial, political and denominational blinders that keep many from seeing Jesus as He is. My prayer for you is that you receive the one revelation that always gets the attention of the Kingdom; the revelation that Jesus is the Christ, Son of the Living God.

In the coming days, it will be critical to know Jesus as the Living Lord, the Christ, the Son of the Living God. Only through Jesus

Christ will we be able to overcome rather than succumb to the enemy's deception and attacks. When you finish reading this book, it is my prayer that you will be able to declare like Peter, "[I] believe and [I am] sure that thou art that Christ, the Son of the living God."[2]

Blessings,

Tim Kurtz
October 2020

---

[2] Paraphrased from John 6:69

...we believe and are sure that thou art that Christ, the Son of the living God.

John 6:69

1 | CAESAREA PHILIPPI

IT BEGAN AT CAESAREA PHILIPPI

What took place at Caesarea Philippi was no random event. It was not just an impromptu side trip taken by Jesus and His disciples after leaving Bethsaida. It was part of a master plan. It was a plan set in motion before the world began. It was a secret plan that was hidden in God, Who made all things by Jesus – the same Jesus Who was leading the disciples on this journey (Ephesians 3:9-11).

> *...to make all men see what is the fellowship of the mystery, WHICH FROM THE BEGINNING OF THE WORLD HATH BEEN HID IN GOD, WHO CREATED ALL THINGS BY JESUS CHRIST: To the intent that now unto the*

1

principalities and powers in heavenly places might be known by the [ekklesia] the manifold wisdom of God, ACCORDING TO THE ETERNAL PURPOSE which he purposed in Christ Jesus our Lord: (Ephesians 3:9-11)

INTRODUCING THE EKKLESIA

The catalyst for the accomplishment of the eternal purpose was a version of a commonly known entity in the first century – the ekklesia. Nearly everyone around Jesus could identify with the ekklesia. It was a group of called out citizens that represented the Roman government in areas relating to local policies, citizenship, legislation and electing officials.

It was at Caesarea Philippi that Jesus would announce His plan to build His version of the ekklesia. His description of its capacity and authority made it clear that it would be a force to be reckoned with. Rather than represent an earthly government, the Lord's ekklesia would represent the Kingdom of Heaven. Just as the citizens who represented Rome had to meet certain criteria, those serving in the Lord's ekklesia would have to meet the necessary criteria of the Kingdom. Then, and only then could they be entrusted to carry out the duties delegated to them.

What is the criteria needed to serve in the Lord's ekklesia? Is the ekklesia open to anyone? How do believers gain access to the ekklesia? How do they appropriate the authority from the Kingdom of Heaven? Answering these and other questions will be covered in this book. Yet, there is one matter that rises above all the others; it is the revelation that Jesus Himself said was mandatory for every believer who is called out to serve Him in His ekklesia.

This book, JESUS CHRIST SON OF THE LIVING GOD, is about understanding the primary revelation every believer needs in order to enter and function in the ekklesia. Jesus said He would build His ekklesia on this one single revelation. This revelation is not just cerebral, but rather a deeply imbedded spiritual truth. It is the revelation necessary to fuel everything we do in behalf of the Kingdom of Heaven.

This revelation is the key to effectively activating the ekklesia as the Lord intended. The question I will seek to answer is, "How do believers get this revelation?" God is not keeping it from you, but this truth has been obscured by years of religious layering. Let's look closely at all that took place at Caesarea Philippi and pay close attention to every detail we can discover.

When Jesus came into the coasts of Caesarea Philippi, he asked his disciples, saying, Whom do men say that I the Son of man am? And they said, Some say that thou art John the Baptist: some, Elias; and others, Jeremias, or one of the prophets. He saith unto them, But whom say ye that I am? And Simon Peter answered and said, Thou art the Christ, the Son of the living God. And Jesus answered and said unto him, Blessed art thou, Simon Barjona: for flesh and blood hath not revealed it unto thee, but my Father which is in heaven. And I say also unto thee, That thou art Peter, and upon this rock I will build my [ekklesia][1]; and the gates

---

[1] Ekklesia is the original Greek word found in ancient text. It has been mistranslated into the English word church.

of hell shall not prevail against it. And I will give unto thee the keys of the king-dom of heaven: and whatsoever thou shalt bind on earth shall be bound in heav-en: and whatsoever thou shalt loose on earth shall be loosed in heaven. Then charged he his disciples that they should tell no man that he was Jesus the Christ. (Matthew 16:13-20)

ARRIVING AT THE COAST

Why Caesarea Philippi? Why was this, of all places, be the place where Jesus would lead His disciples. As we read the conversation Jesus and the disciples had, you would think that it would have been just as appropriate for them to discuss this matter in one of the several homes they visited. They could have discussed this while in route to Capernaum where they ended this journey. But Jesus chose Caesarea Philippi to have this conversation.

Jesus and the disciples were in Bethsaida (Mark 8:22). They left there and went into the cities of Caesarea Philippi (Matthew 16:13; Mark 8:27), then on to Mount Hermon (Matthew 17:1; Mark 9:2). It appears they spent some time in the region of Galilee, and from there they took the journey to Capernaum (Matthew 17:22-24). Without looking at a map of that region, you can easily miss what makes this journey unique.

Bethsaida, where they began was about six miles east of Ca-pernaum where they ended up. Caesarea Philippi was about twen-ty miles north of Bethsaida. Jesus and the disciples literally headed

4

to a place that was twenty miles out of the way – and remember, they were walking.

Caesarea Philippi was a strategic place. For Jesus, it wasn't just another place to visit. To understand its significance, we need to look briefly into the history of this region.

In the first century, Caesarea Philippi was a place oozing with debauchery, paganism and occultism. The external sights and sounds were an outward manifestation of deeper issues taking place in the spirit realm. The spirits who were represented by those purposely participating in the activities at Caesarea Philippi were about to be confronted. In this place Jesus would throw down the gauntlet, challenging the deep underworld. Above all, the restoration of the eternal purpose was about to be declared. This ultimately was central to why Jesus chose this place.

ANOTHER TIME BUT THE SAME PLACE

Psalms 22 is an interesting chapter. Many theologians concur that it paints a vivid Old Testament picture of the crucifixion. Take note of these passages that parallel New Testament text.

> *All they that see me laugh me to scorn: they shoot out the lip, they shake the head, saying, He trusted on the LORD that he would deliver him: let him deliver him, seeing he delighted in him. (Psalms 22:7-8)*

> *Likewise also the chief priests mocking him, with the scribes and elders, said, He saved others; himself he cannot save. If he be the King of Israel, let him now come*

down from the cross, and we will believe him. He trusted in God; let him deliver him now, if he will have him: for he said, I am the Son of God. (Matthew 27:41-43)

I am poured out like water, and all my bones are out of joint: my heart is like wax; it is melted in the midst of my bowels. My strength is dried up like a potsherd; and my tongue cleaveth to my jaws; and thou hast brought me into the dust of death. For dogs have compassed me: the assembly of the wicked have inclosed me: they pierced my hands and my feet. I may tell all my bones: they look and stare upon me. They part my garments among them, and cast lots upon my vesture. (Psalms 22:14-18)

Then the soldiers, when they had crucified Jesus, took his garments, and made four parts, to every soldier a part; and also his coat: now the coat was without seam, woven from the top throughout. They said therefore among themselves, Let us not rend it, but cast lots for it, whose it shall be: that the scripture might be fulfilled, which saith, They parted my raiment among them, and for my vesture they did cast lots. These things therefore the soldiers did. (John 19:23-24)

The similarities in these passages from Psalms 22, Matthew 27 and John 19 are undeniable. Psalms 68 also has language found in the New Testament that refer to a post-resurrection event. Again, you will see the similarities in both texts.

Thou hast ascended on high, thou hast led captivity captive: thou hast received gifts for men; yea, for the rebellious also, that the LORD God might dwell among them. (Psalms 68:18)

Wherefore he saith, When he ascended up on high, he led captivity captive, and gave gifts unto men. (Ephesians 4:8)

Even with the difference of receiving gifts in Psalms 68 and giving gifts in Ephesians 4, there is no ambiguity between these two scriptures. Captivity is led captive. Victory is realized. God wins.

In both Psalms 22 and 68 there is another common thread. They both mention Bashan. On the surface this may not mean much to you, but I want to show its significance to our discussion relating to Caesarea Philippi.

> *Be not far from me, for trouble is near; For there is none to help. Many bulls have surrounded me; Strong bulls of Bashan have encircled me. (Psalms 22:11-12 New American Standard Bible)*

> *A mountain of God is the mountain of Bashan; A mountain of many peaks is the mountain of Bashan. Why do you look with envy, O mountains with many peaks, At the mountain which God has desired for His abode? Surely, the LORD will dwell there forever. (Psalms 68:15-16 New American Standard Bible)*

In Psalms 22 there is a plea for help. The bulls of Bashan encircle the writer in what they believe to be a victory lap. But in Psalms 68, God declares ownership of the mountain of Bashan. He desired to have it for His dwelling place. The mountain of Bashan looked with envy at God's other dwelling place, Mount Sinai. In the end, the mountain of Bashan is conquered as 'captivity is led captive' (Psalms 68:17-18). What does Bashan have to do with all of this?

Bashan was a territory ruled by Og. It was where the remnant of the giants lived (Numbers 21:33; Deuteronomy 3:1; Joshua 13:12). Moses destroyed them at Edrei. These giants were descendants of the giants referenced in Genesis 6:1-4.

> *And it came to pass, when men began to multiply on the face of the earth, and daughters were born unto them, That the sons of God saw the daughters of men that they were fair; and they took them wives of all which they chose. And the LORD said, My spirit shall not always strive with man, for that he also is flesh: yet his days shall be an hundred and twenty years. There were giants in the earth in those days; and also after that, when the sons of God came in unto the daughters of men, and they bare children to them, the same became mighty men which were of old, men of renown.*

There is significant theological debate regarding the sons of God in this text. Were they demonic or divine? I believe they were demonic. The scope of this book will not delve into that aspect of this scripture, but rather point to the giants who were the children of this union. The Nephilim, Rephaim, Zuzim, Emim and even the Amorites were clans of giants, and generally not mentioned in a positive light throughout scripture. Additionally, ancient manuscripts, including the Book of Enoch show the Genesis 6 narrative as the place of demonic intrusion into the earth.

Og The Amorite

Og, the Amorite was an enemy of Israel. He ruled the territory known in ancient Israel as Bashan. Where was Bashan? Once again when you look at an early map, you will see its northern border was Mount Herman. Its southern border was at the northern tip of Gad. On the northern west, it butted up to Canaan and the Sea of Galilee. According to Dr. Michael Heiser[2], this region was known by ancient Israel as the place where 'the gates of hell' existed. In essence it was the access point for demonic intrusion into the earth. In those days it was known as Bashan. In Jesus' day, it was this same area that had become known as Caesarea Philippi.

The demonic atmosphere had not changed. The vulgar temple of the goat god Pan was there; the temple of the Caesars was there; and a cave where human and animal sacrifices took place was there. That cave was referred to in Jesus' day as the gate of Hades.

Remember Mount Herman? This is where the ancient Israelites believed that rebellious 'sons of God' chose to initiate their demonic attack into the earth[3]. But Mount Hermon is also the place where Jesus was transfigured.

Here is the point I want you to see and understand. Caesarea Philippi was no happenstance journey for Jesus and the disciples. It was an 'in your face' encounter with the demonic realm. When Jesus asked how the people saw Him, the answer revealed a religious view of Who He was. But when He asked the same question to the disciples, Peter's response was the revelatory view of Jesus

---

[2] See THE UNSEEN REALM: *Recovering the Supernatural Worldview of the Bible* © 2015 by Michael S. Heiser Published by Lexham Press Pages 282-287

[3] Genesis 6:1-4

Christ. "You are the Christ, Son of the Living God" was the first time there was a clear articulation of His identity.

A few days later, Jesus, along with Peter, James and John made their way up Mount Hermon where He was transfigured before them. Mount Hermon, the very place where it was believed the rebellious 'sons of God' entered the earth, God declared from the heavens, "This (Jesus), is MY beloved Son, in whom I am well pleased, hear him!" The rebellious 'sons' were put on notice, and all the universe was commanded to hear only the voice of Jesus. Jesus knew He was about to go to war.

Matthew, Mark and Luke record similar versions of the transfiguration and the events that followed. However, Luke made an observation not found in the other two gospels.

> *And it came to pass, when the time was come that he should be received up, he stedfastly set his face to go to Jerusalem, (Luke 9:51)*

Jesus was on a mission. He knew He had to get to Jerusalem. He knew the atmosphere was set for the host of hell to take their best shot at Him. He was ready to give His life to reverse the effect caused by the rebellion of the first Adam (1Corinthians 15:45-49). The demonic realm had no idea they had been set up (1Corinthians 2:8). The Pharisees who would arrest and subsequently force the crucifixion were blind pawns of the demonic realm being used to carry out hell's attempt to destroy Jesus. That is why, while suffering on the cross, He asked God to forgive these religious rulers because they had no clue as to what they were doing (Luke 23:34; Acts 3:17).

The seemingly out of the way trip to Caesarea Philippi was divinely orchestrated to position you and I for victory. Death had reigned unchallenged from the rebellion of Adam (Romans 5:14-21). At Caesarea Philippi the imminent defeat of Hades was declared as men received the revelation that Jesus is the Christ, Son of the Living God. Nothing would prevail against the Lord's ekklesia (Matthew 16:15-18). A few days later, on Mount Hermon, the significant roles of Elijah and Moses were aligned so that the supreme reign of Christ could manifest eternally[4]. As you discover more about the life of Jesus, the events surrounding Caesarea Philippi and Mount Hermon will lay a greater foundation for you. No doubt, the revelation that He is the Christ, Son of the Living God will become more of a reality in you.

Over two thousand years have elapsed since the resurrection of Jesus Christ. Many of the historical factors surrounding this event have been either buried in religious rhetoric or diluted over time. Consequently, our view of Jesus Christ can be distorted. You cannot have the revelation of who He is, if you have a dysfunctional view of Him. In the next two chapters, I will begin the process of clarifying the Jesus of scripture. I pray that you will get to know Jesus in a far greater dimension.

---

[4] A study of 'the two olive trees' mentioned in Zechariah 4:11 and Revelation 11:4, along with the transfiguration narrative in Matthew 17, Mark 9, and Luke 9 will show both Elijah and Moses with Jesus. In the Zechariah they were symbolized by the two olive trees, in Revelation 11:6 they are identified by their historical attributes. In both Zechariah and Revelation they were 'standing by' the Lord of the whole earth as seen in the three gospel versions of the transfiguration.

2 | Another Jesus

Jesus said that He would build His ekklesia with those who had the revelation that He is the Christ, Son of the Living God. The ekklesia cannot function with those who only have an academic understanding of who He is. It is necessary to have a deeply imbedded spiritual 'knowing in your knower'. This is what empowers both individuals and the whole ekklesia.

Revelation comes from the throne of God. This book can only point you in a direction, but it cannot produce the revelation that empowers you. Why then is this book necessary? Because too many believers have settled for versions of Jesus that do not fully align with who He is. Many have a religious understanding of Jesus, without an experiential reality of His existence. Countless believers have embraced a denominational view of Jesus, that conflicts with the Jesus of another denomination.

The sons of Sceva tried to cast out a devil in the name of a Jesus they only knew by proxy. Versions of the sons of Sceva still exist today.

Paul alluded to the reality that other versions of Jesus have been preached. Within what he wrote to the Corinthians we discover why many good believers fail to see Jesus as He is.

> But I fear, lest by any means, as the serpent beguiled Eve through his subtilty, so your minds should be corrupted from the simplicity that is in Christ. For if he that cometh preacheth another Jesus, whom we have not preached, or if ye receive another spirit, which ye have not received, or another gospel, which ye have not accepted, ye might well bear with him. (2Corinthians 11:3-4)

The source of a corrupted mind is deception. It is a repeat of falling for the idea that something forbidden by God can make you wise (Genesis 3:6). It is using religious complexity to corrupt the mind from the simplicity in Christ. Religious complexity breeds confusion.

Simplicity is not the same as being frivolous. Simplicity ensures that Christ is available to all. The illiterate and the intellectual have the same access to the power of the resurrected Lord. The corruption Paul warned the Corinthians to avoid was a form of religious intellectualism that was only accessible by an elite few.

There are three factors that breed this error. They are 'another Jesus', 'another spirit', and 'another gospel'.

ANOTHER JESUS

First is the preaching of 'another Jesus'. Denominations are divided by doctrinal distinctions. This results in versions of Jesus that fit the distinction of various groups. We publicly say that we all serve the same Lord, but in reality, the 'Jesus' of one denomination is different from the 'Jesus' of another denomination.

Is Christ divided? In one denomination Jesus Christ is portrayed as a strict guardian of the law. In their version of Jesus, He is intently watching believers to pounce on, and punish any infraction. I have seen believers in such denominations live in constant fear of error. In one case, I knew a person that went years without receiving communion because they kept a list of personal sins they felt disqualified them. They had been taught that based on 1Corinthians 11:29 that they were unworthy of the Lord's Table. When they finally chose to leave that church, they were threatened by the pastor. He told them that because they left, all their family would meet with tragic and untimely death. In essence that pastor cursed them. It took years for this person to gain a biblical view of Jesus.

Another denomination I am familiar with preaches a similar version of Jesus. With them, there are a myriad of laws that determine if a person is saved. Dress codes, prohibiting members from watching television, being strictly forbidden from attending other 'churches', no jewelry or make-up, mandatory attendance to every service, and more such laws are used to determine salvation.

Ironically, many of those I have encountered from this denomination are not as fearful as they are arrogant. They believe that their approach to holiness is superior to all others. They refer to every religious group outside of theirs as Babylon. Some find the courage to break away from this denomination. Sadly, many of them no longer participate in any Christ centered fellowships. They are bitter and avoid believers as much as possible.

On the other extreme, there is another 'church' in my area that is unaffiliated with any denomination. They teach a carnal freedom in Christ. Many, but not all of those who attend this group constantly cross moral lines to prove their 'freedom in Christ'. To them, this equates to the so-called freedom to drink alcohol, party excessively, use colorful language when they desire, and to dress provocatively.

They constantly remind others that 'Christ has redeemed them from the curse of the law'. They claim their life in Christ has made them 'free from the law of sin and death.' On the surface this sounds good. But when you dig deeper, you will discover their view of the 'law', specifically, the 'law of sin and death' is anything that places boundaries on any carnal pleasures. This creates a gross misinterpretation of scripture that suggests modesty, temperance and character as the 'law' they have been freed from.

Jesus is the Word of God made flesh (John 1:14; 1Timothy 3:16). Jesus declared that all scripture points to Him (John 5:39; Luke 24:27). Paul's warning against those who preach another Jesus is not just our contemporary labeling of cult religions. It is any preaching that portrays Jesus in any manner that conflicts with scripture. When 'another Jesus' is preached, it creates 'another spirit' within the adherents of that version of Him.

ANOTHER SPIRIT

To receive 'another spirit' suggests there is a conflict with the spirit we should have as believers. Whatever you internalize, you eventually will materialize. Your lifestyle will reflect your deep-seated beliefs.

In the last section, I shared how a version of Jesus as a disciplinarian created fear. The Jesus of law and restrictions produced arrogance. The Jesus of unbiblical 'freedom' produced ungodly living. Each version of Jesus was reflected in the lives of the believers involved. If these are a reflection of erroneous teaching, what is the correct spirit that should be evident in believers?

Paul's admonition to the Corinthians was clear. They had received 'another spirit' that was different from the Spirit they had originally received. Throughout his letters to them, we see the Corinthians had a constant battle with carnality.

There were factions among them like the denominational factions today (1Corinthians 1:12). This resulted in immaturity made obvious by their envying, strife and divisions (1Corinthians 3:1-4). They had erroneously elevated those who taught them (1Corinthians 4:1-6). They could not accurately deal with sin within their ranks. They showed no capacity to deal with disputes. They lacked wisdom in handling marital issues. They foolishly glorified spiritual gifts. As you read Paul's two letters to the Corinthians, it is clear they had serious issues. Their dysfunction can be found among believers today. This leads me to conclude that much of what we label as Christianity today reflects 'another spirit'.

> *But you are not in the flesh but in the Spirit, if indeed the Spirit of God dwells in you. Now if anyone does not have the Spirit of Christ, he is not His. And if Christ is in you, the body is dead because of sin, but the Spirit is life because of righteousness. But if the Spirit of Him who raised Jesus from the dead dwells in you, He who raised Christ from the dead will also give life to your mortal bodies through His Spirit who dwells in you. (Romans 8:9-11 New King James Version)*

Everything we do should point to Jesus Christ. Everything we are should emanate from Him alone. Our public image reflects our inward reality. Without the Sprit of Christ, we do not belong to Him. There is nothing ambiguous about that statement. You either are, or you aren't His. You either have, or you don't have the Spirit of Christ. When we confess that Jesus is the Christ, Son of the Living God, our life must reflect the Spirit of Christ dwelling in us.

Otherwise, it becomes evident that we have succumbed to 'another spirit'.

ANOTHER GOSPEL

The third factor is the preaching of 'another gospel'. How can there be 'another gospel' when the gospel is supposed to be 'the good news'?

The woman in the Garden was deceived by satan. Deception is the corruption of truth. Another gospel is changing the good news into something that sounds good. Instead of pointing to Christ, it appeases the desires of the flesh. It interprets the Word of God with human wisdom.

> *Now the serpent was more subtil than any beast of the field which the LORD God had made. And he said unto the woman, Yea, hath God said, Ye shall not eat of every tree of the garden? And the woman said unto the serpent, We may eat of the fruit of the trees of the garden: But of the fruit of the tree which is in the midst of the garden, God hath said, Ye shall not eat of it, neither shall ye touch it, lest ye die. And the serpent said unto the woman, Ye shall not surely die: For God doth know that in the day ye eat thereof, then your eyes shall be opened, and ye shall be as gods, knowing good and evil. And when the woman saw that the tree was good for food, and that it was pleasant to the eyes, and a tree to be desired to make one wise, she took of the fruit thereof, and did eat, and gave also unto her husband with her; and he did eat. (Genesis 3:1-6)*

Notice in this passage that the devil did not deny what God had said, instead he redefined it. He suggested that dying was an attempt by God to keep them ignorant of what good and evil was all about. Immediately the woman's perception of the tree changed. She saw it as good for food, like every other tree in the Garden (Genesis 3:2-3). This made the tree pleasant to the eyes. Her imagination took her outside of God and into herself. And finally, she concluded that it would produce wisdom that would be equal to God. This became her reasoning for eating.

Her husband evidently did not see any damage done, so he too ate of the tree. It was at this point that their eyes were opened. It was after eating of the tree that they saw themselves as naked. I often noted that they were naked before they ate, but now their view of that nakedness was corrupted. They saw themselves as being exposed. What they did next reinforces what happens when a person succumbs to the preaching of 'another gospel'.

> *And the eyes of them both were opened, and they knew that they were naked; and they sewed fig leaves together, and made themselves aprons. (Genesis 3:7)*

They attempted to cover their nakedness. Let's look closer into this futile act.

First, they did not make hats to cover their heads. I believe that would have suggested they understood their thoughts were corrupted. Second, they did not make gloves to cover their hands. Gloves may imply that they knew their actions were in error.

Third, they did not make sandals or something to cover their feet implying they knew the path they were on was wrong. Instead they made aprons.

Aprons cover the mid-body, specifically the genital area. I have concluded that this implies they knew they could only reproduce what they had become – human beings who would be estranged from God. The aprons are a form of human covering of sin.

Religion is man's attempt to find God. Although Jesus declared He is the Way, the Truth and the Life, mankind is still trying to find God on their own terms (John 14:6). They are still making aprons to cover themselves. They remove their religious aprons long enough to produce more error in generation after generation. This becomes the strength of another gospel.

GOOD AND EVIL

Why was the tree of the Knowledge of Good and Evil off limits? I pondered over why God would plant a tree in His garden, and then tell the man and woman it was not to be touched.

Over the years I have heard many answers to this issue. They ranged from God just wanting to test man's obedience, to the tree being a form of the tithe that belonged to God. I believe these conclusions fall short of a greater reason.

And the LORD God said, Behold, the man is become as one of us, to know good and evil: and now, lest he put forth his hand, and take also of the tree of life, and eat, and live for ever: (Genesis 3:22)

One of the most poignant statements regarding good and evil came soon after man had disobeyed God. Remember, immediately after they had sinned, their eyes were opened. They had an entirely different perspective of themselves, their environment and God. Their assignment to represent God in the earth was gone. The Garden was to have been their place of safety. Within it was the Tree of Life. If they had partaken of it, they would live forever. The problem is that they would live forever in an eternal state of corruption.

God had determined to redeem man from their sin and restore them back to His intended purpose. When He drove man out of the Garden, it was not a punitive response, but rather a protective act (Genesis 3:23-24). By keeping them away from the Tree of Life, He insured that man would not be eternally lost. Scripture reveals that the Tree of Life is waiting for anyone who overcomes and follows God's commandments (Revelation 22:2, 14). But what about the Tree of the Knowledge of Good and Evil?

The way Genesis 3:22 is worded in the King James and other translations, it appears that man gained the knowledge of good and evil after they partook of the tree. This can be confusing. The Septuagint, which is the Greek translation of the Old Testament clarifies this matter. It says that, *"Adam was made like one of us to know good and evil."* In other words, from the beginning, man was created in the image and likeness of God. Within man was the capacity to know good and evil, however, he had to learn how to use it.

Throughout all scripture is reference after reference of men doing evil, and believing they are doing good. The prophet Isaiah declared, *"Woe unto them that call evil good, and good evil; that put darkness for light, and light for darkness; that put bitter for sweet, and sweet for bitter!"* (Isaiah 5:20). There are some who persecute the people of God and believe they are doing God's will (John 16:2). Their minds are so corrupted that they are pleased by those who do evil (Romans 1:21-32). A corrupt mind and spirit cannot accurately determine what is good and what is evil.

> For when for the time ye ought to be teachers, ye have need that one teach you again which be the first principles of the oracles of God; and are become such as have need of milk, and not of strong meat. For every one that useth milk is unskilful in the word of righteousness: for he is a babe. But strong meat belongeth to them that are of full age, **even those who by reason of use have their senses exercised to discern both good and evil** (Hebrews 5:12-14)

The ability to discern what is good and what is evil requires training the senses. Because something feels good, does not mean it is good in the sight of God. God's purpose is good, but His purpose is not determined by how we feel. Everything the woman saw in the tree appeared to be good. Her and her husband's disobedi-

23

ence revealed their immaturity. They would have learned more by obeying God.

The Tree of the Knowledge of Good and Evil was a point of training. It may have been pleasant to look at. It could have been good for food. The lure of wisdom could have been present (1John 2:15-16). But to partake of it prematurely was willful disobedience, and everything it appeared to be would be immediately nullified. This is the foundation of 'another gospel'.

IDENTITY GOSPEL

Whenever a form of gospel is labeled, it suggests a potential version that does not line up with the gospel of Jesus Christ or the gospel of His kingdom (Matthew 4:23; 1Corinthians 15:1-4; Galatians 1:10-12). These gospel variations can be recognized by the over emphasis of an ideology. The prosperity gospel, the hyper-faith gospel, culturally distinctive gospel, social gospel, or political gospel have become versions of 'another gospel' being preached. Proponents of these distinctions do not create or label themselves, but rather their primary message makes it easy to recognize the heart of their gospel.

On the surface, Jesus Christ is presented as the source of salvation. That is good, until you realize that salvation is mingled with the identity of the gospel that has been preached. In other words, a person receives Jesus Christ because they have been taught that worldly prosperity is godly (1Timothy 6:5). They accept Jesus Christ because He has been framed in context of a social or political movement. In worse case scenarios, Jesus Christ is preached to support racial divisions. Those who embrace these variant gospels rarely realize they are being led down a path to destruction.

What makes these gospels so dangerous? It is how they manipulate the Word of God to support a narrative. Scriptures are cut and pasted together to create pseudo-doctrines. These doctrines build belief systems that appeal to the carnal nature. Why would people be attracted to these aberrations of the gospel? Paul suggested that it was a result of being enamored with the source rather than the substance of the gospel. The Corinthians had tolerated those who came preaching another gospel. They were willing to bear with their false teachings (1Corinthians 11:4). Paul also confronted the issue of 'another gospel' with the Galatians.

> *I marvel that ye are so soon removed from him that called you into the grace of Christ unto another gospel: Which is not another; but there be some that trouble you, and would pervert the gospel of Christ. But though we, or an angel from heaven, preach any other gospel unto you than that which we have preached unto you, let him be accursed. As we said before, so say I now again, If any man preach any other gospel unto you than that ye have received, let him be accursed. (Galatians 1:6-9)*

Paul issued a stern warning that anyone who preached another gospel should be considered accursed. He was so serious about this that he included himself. This leaves no doubt that the gospel of Jesus Christ was not to be compromised. The perversion of the gospel is not to be tolerated.

Remember that the preaching of 'another Jesus' creates 'another spirit' in people. The revelation that Jesus is the Christ, Son of the Living God can be tainted by distorted doctrine. As I have said earlier, and will say again now, doctrine is provided to clarify a value. A value is often an unspoken belief that underscores why certain actions are taken. It is reflected in what is said. It is one of the things that in essence, 'go without being said'.

> Moreover, brethren, I declare unto you the gospel which I preached unto you, which also ye have received, and wherein ye stand; By which also ye are saved, if ye keep in memory what I preached unto you, unless ye have believed in vain. For I delivered unto you first of all that which I also received, how that Christ died for our sins according to the scriptures; And that he was buried, and that he rose again the third day according to the scriptures: (1Corinthians 15:1-4)

Paul in his discourse to the Corinthians clarified the first primary value of the Kingdom – the Lordship of Jesus Christ. He made sure they understood the gospel that had been preached to them, as well as the 'Jesus' within that gospel. He left no room for 'another Jesus'. The only gospel that saves and provides a foundation on which we stand, is the gospel that speaks of the life, death, burial and resurrection of Jesus Christ – according to the scriptures. It is when we embrace Jesus, according to the scriptures – that we can have any hope of positioning ourselves to receive the revelation that He is the Christ, Son of the Living God!

3 | He Knows My Name

Jesus is the Christ – Son of the Living God. Say it out loud. Jesus is the Christ – Son of the Living God. Again. Jesus is the Christ – Son of the Living God. Hearing yourself say it will begin to anchor this truth in your spirit. Saying it is the easy part. Proof of this becoming a revelation in you is not in the ability to declare it, but rather how this truth manifests in your life.

In chapter **9**, I will give you a greater understanding of what a revelation is. When you live with the revelation of Christ being the Son of God, you will not second guess what you do. Any speck of doubt will cause you to draw back in times of temptation.

> And these signs shall follow them that believe; In my name shall they cast out devils; they shall speak with new tongues; They shall take up serpents; and if they drink any deadly thing, it shall not hurt them; they shall lay hands on the sick, and they shall recover. (Mark 16:17-18)

Signs follow 'them that believe'. What do they believe? Jesus states that it is IN HIS NAME devils are cast out, new tongues are spoken, dominion is exercised over serpents, poisons become ineffective, and the sick are healed by the laying on of hands. These are very specific signs He said would follow believers. Yet, look around you. For the majority of Christians, these signs are noticeably absent in their daily experience. Why is this? I suggest the answer is as simple as it is poignant. There is an absence of believers.

Let me be clear. There are many who have confessed Jesus as Lord but have not fully grasped the revelation that He is the Christ, Son of the Living God. Many have accepted the persona of Jesus Christ, more than the person of Jesus Christ. They live each day based on moral goodness, which they should do, but that is not the total picture.

Others believe Jesus from historical evidence, theological teachings and denominational doctrine. These have their place, but often fall short in times of trouble. Their inability to produce the signs stated by Jesus Christ imply that something in what they believe is missing.

If you believe the Word of God, you can't get around what it says. Signs follow believers. The lack of the signs Jesus listed suggest the absence of believers. However, to focus solely on the signs will cause you to miss what Jesus said. Signs alone are not the total picture.

I believe that miraculous signs should be a common reality among believers. We should live supernatural lives, always ready to release the power of the resurrected Lord in any situation. The result will be the manifestation of signs. But we must also be careful not to idolize the signs. The signs should validate the presence of the Risen King, rather than draw attention to us.

> Not every one that saith unto me, Lord, Lord, shall enter into the kingdom of heaven; but he that doeth the will of my Father which is in heaven. Many will say to me in that day, Lord, Lord, have we not prophesied in thy name? and in thy name have cast out devils? and in thy name done many wonderful works? And then will I profess unto them, I never knew you: depart from me, ye that work iniquity. (Matthew 7:21-23)

We are all familiar with Jesus' teaching regarding those who prophesied, cast out devils and did many wonderful works in His Name only to have Him say that He never knew them. He called them workers of iniquity. That is a pretty tough indictment against people who on the surface appeared to be doing good things. Even their appeal to Jesus was based on the works they had done. "Have we not prophesied in your name? Have we not cast out devils in your name? Haven't we done many wonderful works?" Aren't these things similar to the signs Jesus said would follow believers?

This posed a dilemma for me as I was researching and writing this book. I had based much of what I taught on this subject on the supernatural works that emanated from having the revelation of Jesus being the Christ, Son of the Living God. Yet, I can't discard what

Jesus said to those who did great works but still fell woefully short. As I read Jesus' words in Matthew 7:23; I saw something that was in plain sight, but I had completely missed its deeper meaning. Jesus said, "...I never knew you".

In my desire to have an unshakeable revelation of who Jesus is, I realized that it is equally important that He knows who I am. It's me knowing Him and Him knowing me that create two sides of the same coin.

> For there shall arise false Christs, and false prophets, and shall shew great signs and wonders; insomuch that, if it were possible, they shall deceive the very elect. (Matthew 24:24)

The disciples asked Jesus to tell them the signs of His return. His answer should make our eschatology simple. "Take heed that no one deceives you!" (Matthew 24:3-4). The rise of deception is the greatest sign of the Lord's return. It is the single most effective tool of the enemy. The lust of the eyes and the pride of life peppered with religious rhetoric have deceived many into believing they are okay. Our western ala carte and consumer driven Christianity deceptively provides a false sense of security.

This leads us back to Jesus warning. He said the rise of false christs and prophets would be accompanied by great signs and wonders. Don't miss this point; signs and wonders can be performed by false ministries. If signs alone are your litmus test for determining the presence of God, you can potentially be deceived.

Misunderstood, signs and wonders can lure some away from the truth.

Jesus said, "I never knew you". This reveals and exposes a truth we must understand. On one side, the Lord would build His ekklesia with those who knew He was the Christ, Son of the Living God. But, on the other hand, it is equally important for the Lord to know those who follow Him. In other words, our works are of no value if the Lord does not claim us. He said such people are workers of iniquity. Some translations say they are workers of lawlessness. Regardless, they were people working outside the boundaries of the Lord's Kingdom. Why is this so important?

THE COST OF BEING KNOWN BY THE LORD

Now great multitudes went with Him. And He turned and said to them, "If anyone comes to Me and does not hate his father and mother, wife and children, brothers and sisters, yes, and his own life also, he cannot be My disciple. And whoever does not bear his cross and come after Me cannot be My disciple. For which of you, intending to build a tower, does not sit down first and count the cost, whether he has enough to finish it -- "lest, after he has laid the foundation, and is not able to finish, all who see it begin to mock him, saying, 'This man began to build and was not able to finish.' Or what king, going to make war against another king, does not sit down first and consider whether he is able with ten thousand to meet him who comes against him with twenty thousand? Or else, while the other is still a great way off, he sends a delegation and asks conditions of peace. So likewise, whoever of you does not forsake all that he has cannot be My disciple. Salt is good; but if the salt has lost its flavor, how shall it be seasoned?

It is neither fit for the land nor for the dunghill, but men throw it out. He who has ears to hear, let him hear!" (Luke 14:25-35 NKJV)

In the first part of this parable, Jesus revealed the high cost of being His disciple. He expects His followers to give up all to follow Him. Later, He asked the multitude two questions that exposed why His disciples must meet His high criteria. They reveal His intent to build and, if necessary, go to war with only those who qualified.

He first asked, "Who among you...?" would attempt to build a tower without sufficient material. It would be futile to lay a foundation only to discover there was inadequate supplies. Then He asked, "What king going to war against another king..." would do so without first determining His military capacity? The answer is that no one in the crowd would attempt either building or going to war under the conditions He outlined.

Jesus then placed the burden on those He was addressing. "So likewise..." Let me say this another way. By saying "so likewise..." Jesus meant, "If YOU wouldn't build or go to war under the conditions I outlined, you can understand that I won't do it either". Jesus was saying that He would build and go to war with only those qualified to be His disciples. No one less than a fully vested disciple would be fit for the Kingdom. Let's go further.

Now when he was in Jerusalem at the Passover, in the feast day, MANY BELIEVED IN HIS NAME, WHEN THEY SAW THE MIRACLES WHICH HE DID. BUT JESUS DID NOT COMMIT HIMSELF UNTO THEM, because he knew all men, (John 2:23-24)

Once again, we see many people claiming to believe in Jesus' name, but only due to the miracles they had seen. Therefore, Jesus did not commit Himself to them. The miracles were their motivation, not Jesus Himself. Many say they have committed themselves to the Lord, but here we see it is equally important that He is committed to them.

This gets back to the reality that signs performed by those unknown to Jesus create the atmosphere for deception. Deception runs deep if it is not exposed. Notice how many people were impacted.

First, there were the recipients of prophetic ministry, second, there were those who had demons cast out of them, and thirdly, there were the people who were the beneficiaries of some wonderful work, and all from people that Jesus declared He did not know. Also, it is not clear from the biblical text if those who performed these signs were fully aware that they were deceived. They had assumed their prophesying, casting out devils and good works were enough (Matthew 7:22). It cannot be overstated that all this deception was exposed to us because Jesus declared He did not know those who performed the signs.

In his letter to the Corinthians, Paul listed nine gifts that were given by the Holy Spirit, which included miracles, prophecy and healing among others. He prefaced this list by admonishing them that they had been 'carried away' with these dumb or mute idols. They were idolizing the gifts (1Corithians 12:1-11). In the next chapter, He concluded by exhorting them to be mature.

But when that which is perfect is come, then that which is in part shall be done away. When I was a child, I spake as a child, I understood as a child, I thought as a child: but when I became a man, I put away childish things. For now we see through a glass, darkly; but then face to face: now I know in part; but then shall I know even as also I am known. (1Corinthians 13:10-12)

Your car is assembled from thousands of parts. I doubt if you get excited over the alternator, or the drive shaft. They have a role to play but they are only parts of the total vehicle. Your sight is on the 'complete' automobile. Likewise, to focus on the miracles, the healings, and the prophecies, you ultimately miss the totality of Jesus Christ. Emphasis on 'parts' is the root of immaturity. To be enamored by the gifts creates the inability to see the giver. When the 'perfect' or the 'complete' is seen, then the parts – that still exist, function in their prescribed place.

"I shall know, even as I am known!" The Bible in Basic English translation says it this way. "...now my knowledge is in part; then it will be complete, *even as God's knowledge of me.*" God's complete knowledge of you is important. Even though you may only know and understand your part, maturity aligns you so that you will be known. That is the key factor. You need to be known by the Lord.

SCEVA-ISM

Too many ministry works are failing because they function in a form of Sceva-ism. They are presumptuous in their abilities; thinking if so and so can do it, so can I. Their defeat is not the result of good

36

intentions, bur rather that they are unknown by both the Lord and demonic spirits. Yes, that's right. The demons know those who are known by the Lord. "Jesus I know, and Paul I know; but who are you?" In other words, they have no authority because they are not known by the Lord (Acts 19:13-16).

Jesus said, "My sheep hear my voice, *and I know them*, and they follow me:" (John 10:27). When the seventy returned proclaiming that demons were subject to them, Jesus said the most important thing was to know that their names were written in heaven (Luke 10:20). It was critical that heaven could identify them.

You can declare that Jesus is the Christ, Son of the Living God, but remember that the very foundation of God stands on the fact that 'the Lord knows those who are His' (2Timothy 2:19).

4 | Revealing Our Motives

Jesus is the Christ, Son of the Living God. This must be more than a religious declaration, it must become a Holy Spirit imbued revelation. It is imperative that you be in Christ, but equally imperative that Christ be in you (2Corinthians 5:17; Colossians 1:27).

In the last chapter we learned that signs follow believers. However, we also discovered that signs can be performed by false christs and false prophets. Jesus declared He had no knowledge of some who had done the very works He said would follow believers. We concluded that the key factor is to be known by Jesus.

As important as it is for Him to know you, in this chapter I want to show the importance of you knowing Jesus as He is. This undergirds my quest to build a strong biblical foundation in you regarding the person of Jesus Christ. This chapter will also help you examine your motives for knowing Jesus. Throughout scripture several people came into contact with Him, and time and time again their true motives were discovered.

I desire that you not be 'barren or unfruitful in the knowledge of our Lord Jesus Christ' (2Peter 1:8). My prayer is that you know Jesus without any religious, ideological or even emotional filters so that you can say unequivocally by the Spirit of God that Jesus is the Christ, Son of the Living God.

A question was poised to Jesus by some of the religious leaders. They seemingly wanted to know how they could do the 'works of God'. The answer Jesus gave them was not what they wanted to hear. They wanted to *do* something; but Jesus said they needed to *believe* something.

The works of God is imbedded in believing who God had sent, not in some external action, religious ritual or spiritualized ceremony. As I looked at their request in the context leading up to it, I believe it revealed they had an ulterior motive. Their question was self-serving and Jesus response exposed their true heart. Let's look at this in detail.

DOING THE RIGHT THING ON THE WRONG DAY

Jesus had upset the Jews when He healed a man on the Sabbath. The religious leaders were so locked into their traditions, that they would prefer a man remain infirmed rather than see him healed on their misguided view of the Sabbath.

At one point they wanted to kill Jesus because of what they deemed to be a Sabbath infraction as well as His claim that God was His Father. Yet, their rhetoric could not override the attention created through the miracle of the lame man being healed (John 5:1-18). Thus, by the time we read into John chapter six, we see multitudes of people following Jesus.

TWO-PIECE FISH DINNER

As He continued to travel throughout the region, many followed him because of the miracles He performed. Jesus saw the multitudes and asked His disciples what could be done to feed them. What was interesting is that the bible states that Jesus knew in advance what He would do (John 6:1-6).

The disciples, probably somewhat sarcastically, produced a meal from a young boy consisting of two fish and five barley loaves. Clearly not enough to feed so many people; but that is exactly what Jesus did. He took the bread, blessed it, brake it and gave it to the disciples to distribute among the people.

Without question, feeding over five thousand people with a two-piece fish dinner was surely a powerful miracle. But was this done solely for the people and the disciples to witness? Did the fact that Jesus knew what He would do in advance suggest that

He also knew His actions would reveal the true heart of some following Him?

> Then those men, when they had seen the sign that Jesus did, said, "This is truly the Prophet who is to come into the world." Therefore when Jesus perceived that they were about to come and take Him by force to make Him king, He departed again to the mountain by Himself alone. (John 6:14-15 NKJV)

The 'those men' mentioned appear to be a group, separate and distinct from the multitude and the disciples. Based on their response to the miracle, I suggest, these were some of the local religious leaders. They determined that Jesus had to be some special prophet. He realized that they wanted to force Him to be their king. Instead He separated Himself from them by going into a mountain alone to pray (John 6:15). He also separated His disciples from them by sending them to the other side of the lake. This set up a second miracle that was only witnessed by the disciples, but is equally significant to this entire series of events.

The disciples encountered a fierce storm as they tried to cross the lake. Jesus saw them struggling and approached them walking on the water. They were frightened, but Jesus reassured them by calming the sea. Matthew's version of this event described Peter's attempt to walk on the water with Jesus (Matthew 14:28-29). According to Mark's version of this event, after Jesus calmed the sea, it appeared the disciples' hearts were hardened; and they did not consider the previous miracle of loaves and fishes (John 6:16-21; Mark 6:47-52).

By the time Jesus and the disciples arrived at the other side of the sea, the multitude who had eaten the loaves and fishes discovered Jesus had left the area. They took some boats to follow Him. I believe that among them were the religious leaders who wanted to force Him to be king. Unlike the disciples who 'did not consider' the miracle of the loaves and fishes, these religious leaders 'did consider' the miracle and wanted to use this for their own advantage.

Jesus did not mince words with the crowd. He said their only reason for following Him was because of the fish dinner they had been given (John 6:22-27). That is when the religious leaders asked Jesus how they could do what He did (i.e. multiply loaves and fish). Don't forget that they previously wanted to force Jesus to be their king. When He showed no interest, they took another approach. If they could learn how to do the 'works of God' they could possibly find a king from among their ranks. It was the conversation that ensued after they had made this request from Jesus that led me to this conclusion.

BREAD FROM HEAVEN

The religious leaders had seen the man healed on the Sabbath. Even though they were angered, they could do nothing about it. This initiated a conversation between them and Jesus regarding doing the works of the Father. Also, take note that Jesus brought their misguided understanding of Moses into the conversation (John 5:17-47). This is significant, because later we will see them trying to justify what they knew about Moses.

> *Then said they unto him, What shall we do, that we might work the works of God? Jesus answered and said unto them, This is the work of God, that ye believe on him whom he hath sent. (John 6:28-29)*

Jesus described the works of God as believing the One Who He had sent. Then the religious leaders wanted Jesus to give them a sign. They specifically gave the example of the manna from heaven the Israelites received under Moses (John 6:30-31). This was not the best example for them to use; but it was the closest thing they had to compare with the loaves and fish miracle.

 Had the religious leaders forgotten the fact that the manna in the wilderness was provision for a fearful, rebellious and murmuring people? Manna was mercy provisions to a people who had refused to enter the land God had promised them. The miracles they witnessed was not enough for them to trust God. Their preference was to die in bondage (Numbers 14). They were turned into the wilderness by God to be purged of a generation of people who had rejected His promise (Numbers 14:29-33).

The religious leaders used the manna as their example to Jesus, but clearly had forgotten, or ignored the fact that Israel murmured against God regarding it (Numbers 11:6; 21:5). To use manna as their example reveals the one-sided view they had. This may be why Jesus compared Himself to the manna. At first, the religious leaders rejected Jesus and wanted to kill Him. Now they wanted to get something from Him for their advantage. So, Jesus declared that He was the bread from heaven that brings life.

The conversation, at least from the religious leaders' perspective, went downhill from that point, especially when Jesus said that it was necessary to eat His flesh and drink His blood to have life. This created conflict among the religious leaders and confusion among those in the crowd. It was just too much for many of them to handle. As a result, many of the disciples stopped following Jesus (John 6:32-66).

> Then said Jesus unto the twelve, Will ye also go away? Then Simon Peter answered him, Lord, to whom shall we go? thou hast the words of eternal life. (John 6:67-68)

Did Jesus try to placate the twelve? Absolutely not. He gave them the opportunity to leave, too. "Where would we go?" Peter asked. That response suggests they had most likely given some advance consideration to this question. They obviously concluded that there was no place to go. It was also at this time that Peter restated the revelation that He received at Caesarea Philippi. At some point before you finish reading this book, I want you to boldly make the same proclamation Peter did; "...I believe and [I'm] sure that [you are] that Christ, the Son of the living God" (John 6:69).

WHAT HAVE WE LEARNED SO FAR?

The preceding reveals how some people see Jesus. The religious leaders wanted to know how to 'work the works of God'. Their motives were not pure. They had been looking for a king, so their purpose was self-promoting.

Today the religious landscape is filled with some who claim to have some specified ministry. People flock to healing ministries, deliverance ministries, and prophetic ministries seeking to get something from the Lord. Too often the faith healer, deliverance minister or prophet appear to be the greatest beneficiary, especially in the realm of financial gain.

I must be clear that I am not suggesting that all these ministers are unscrupulous. Without a doubt most are sincere but there are those who use the gifts and calling of God for personal gain (Romans 11:29). Unfortunately, the bad ones keep cropping up in such a way that they taint the publics view of the miracle working power of God.

Those who follow these ministries are often disillusioned when their favorite minister falls or fails. How can such an anointed person fall into sexual sin or get caught in some financial scandal? Why did they use trickery to make us believe they were working miracles? Of course, such antics cause many to abandon these false ministries. The greater damage is that the person who wanted to believe so much, will end up with a tainted view of God, and in worse cases, will leave the faith altogether.

As of this writing, we are still in the beginning of a season dubbed 'the day of the Saints'. The works of God will less and less be limited to special services. Ordinary believers will prophesy, cast out devils, and lay hands on the sick. As a need arises, they will respond with the resurrected power of Jesus Christ. These saints of God will not carry titles or be known for great public ministries. They will be like you and I who simply believe. Believe what? That Jesus is the Christ, Son of the Living God.

AS HE IS...

Every Christian loves Jesus. At least they love their version of Him. The vast majority of Christendom's love for the Lord is filtered through the lens of their denominational portrayal of Him. Yes, they generally love Jesus, but it is necessary to strengthen that love by challenging what may be false conclusions of who He is.

> Herein is our love made perfect, that we may have boldness in the day of judgment: because as he is, so are we in this world. (1John 4:17)

Scripture asserts that 'as Jesus is – so are we in this world'. Often we limit this to moral conduct. We generally believe to be like Jesus we must be a good person, with good character, and have gentle behavior. But you can find atheist who fit that criteria. What makes us different?

Our quest should be to emulate Jesus Christ in authority over sin (Romans 6:9-12; Hebrews 4:15). We should be like Him when confronted with sickness and disease (Mark 16:17-18; Luke 10:19; John 14:12). This is the heart of what it means to be as He is in this world. Otherwise, our view as well as our relationship with Him will be subject to shifting.

I am struck by the number of times in scripture when people adored Jesus in one moment and turned totally against Him in the next. Here are three examples.

Look what happened the first time Jesus shared in the synagogue. What began as a glowing overview of Isaiah 61, ended in confrontation.

> *And [Jesus] began to say unto them, This day is this scripture fulfilled in your ears. And all bare him witness, and wondered at the gracious words which proceeded out of his mouth. And they said, Is not this Joseph's son? (Luke 4:21-22)*

A few moments later...

> *And all they in the synagogue, when they heard these things, were filled with wrath, And rose up, and thrust him out of the city, and led him unto the brow of the hill whereon their city was built, that they might cast him down headlong. (Luke 4:28-29)*

Earlier we saw what happened after Jesus had fed the five thousand. People gladly followed Him until their motives were challenged.

> *When the people therefore saw that Jesus was not there, neither his disciples, they also took shipping, and came to Capernaum, seeking for Jesus. And when they*

had found him on the other side of the sea, they said unto him, Rabbi, when cam-
est thou hither? (John 6:24-25)

Again, it only took a few moments for things to change...

Many therefore of his disciples, when they had heard this, said, This is an hard
saying; who can hear it? (John 6:60)

From that time many of his disciples went back, and walked no more with
him. (John 6:66)

Finally, the week before He was crucified, Jesus entered Jerusalem being worshipped and adored by the multitudes.

And the multitudes that went before, and that followed, cried, saying, Hosanna
to the Son of David: Blessed is he that cometh in the name of the Lord; Hosanna
in the highest. And when he was come into Jerusalem, all the city was moved, say-
ing, Who is this? And the multitude said, This is Jesus the prophet of Nazareth of
Galilee. (Matthew 21:9-11)

About one week later...

And Pilate answered and said again unto them, What will ye then that I shall do
unto him whom ye call the King of the Jews? And they cried out again, Crucify
him. Then Pilate said unto them, Why, what evil hath he done? And they cried out
the more exceedingly, Crucify him. (Mark 15:12-14)

I can guarantee that those who abruptly switched their opinion of Jesus did not have the revelation of who He was. He was ac-
ceptable and desired as long as He met some soulish or fleshly de-

sire they had. The moment He challenged them in any way, they quickly turned against Him. This reveals an important matter for you to grasp. You must receive Jesus on His terms – not yours.

God loves us and calls us sons. Our sonship is based on the fact that we must see Jesus 'as He is' (1John 3:2). Paul revealed that there are those who preach 'another Jesus' (2Corinthians 11:4). And even during one of His imprisonments, there were some preaching variations of Christ (Philippians 1:14-17). Even a partial message can have a negative impact on what we believe about Jesus.

GOOD INTENTIONS WRONG MESSAGE

Apollos was an eloquent speaker. His heart was in the right place, but his message was incomplete. While in Ephesus, he preached from the scriptures the baptism of John simply because that is all he knew. Aquila and Priscilla heard him, and quietly took him aside and explained to him 'the way of God more perfectly'. When his understanding was enlightened, he went into Achaia convincing the Jews by the scriptures, that Jesus was the Christ (Acts 18:24-28).

The impact of Apollos' previously incomplete teaching was seen when Paul came to Ephesus. There he came across certain disciples. The fact that they are identified as 'certain' disciples implies these were most likely among those who had been taught by Apollos. Paul's line of questioning appears to confirm this.

"Have you received the Holy Ghost since you believed?" It turned out these believers had never heard of the Holy Ghost. Paul's next question to them on the surface seemed out of place. Rather than laying hands on them to be filled with the Holy Ghost; Paul asked them, "How were you baptized?" They answered, "With John's baptism". Paul then shared with them the difference between John's baptism and the baptism in Jesus' name. It was after this that these disciples received the Holy Ghost (Acts 19:1-7)

I share this story because the underlying truth in this episode proves that what we have been taught about Jesus impacts what we receive from Him. Even though his intentions were good, Apollos had taught these Ephesian disciples a gospel that had left them without a complete view of Jesus Christ. That is why when Paul met them, they had no understanding of the Holy Ghost.

This applies to you and I. If we have been taught an incomplete gospel, we can potentially miss out on all that the Lord has for us. If our view of Jesus is based solely on an emotional or physical benefit we receive, then in times of conflict and challenge we are subject to 'no longer walk with Him'. If we want to 'work the works of God' without really knowing Who God has sent, we can become self-promoting and disingenuous in our relationship with Him.

What have you learned about Jesus? Is your view of Him limited to what a denomination, a culture, or even an ideology has described Him to be? Like Apollos, their intentions may be good, but has their limited view of Jesus our Lord weakened your spiritual growth? This may be hard for you to answer, as most of us believe we really know Jesus. Therefore, a challenge to our view of our Lord is a necessary step towards embracing Him as He is.

5 | Exploring His Deity: Birth, Life and Death

Jesus is the Christ, Son of the Living God.

Any unanswered questions you have about who He is can keep you from fully embracing this reality. Any false assumptions about Him can cause you to 'be ashamed of Him' when things are said that you can't confidently refute (Mark 8:38). We are admonished to sanctify the Lord God in our hearts for the purpose of answering anyone who asks of the hope within us (1Peter 3:15). Therefore, you should desire God to reveal His Son to you (Galatians 1:15-16).

In this chapter I will give you a general overview of the deity of Jesus Christ. This is not intended to be a full-fledged apologetic treatise on this subject. My purpose is to give you some general, but necessary foundational facts. There are five key factors relating to the life of Jesus Christ. They are, (1) His virgin birth, (2) His sinless life, (3) His vicarious death, (4) His bodily resurrection and (5) His bodily return.

I encourage you to study these further. Throughout my thirty-five plus years in ministry, I have found that non-Christian groups can easily be identified based on their distorted view of one or more of these five factors. First, allow me to share how I learned them.

TWO LESSONS LEARNED

In the 1970's I miraculously received a job in my county's Department of Social Services. At that time, I was a new believer and excited to share what I knew about the Lord. Among my co-workers was a Jehovah's Witness. During our lunch break one day she challenged my faith. A group of other co-workers quickly surrounded us as the verbal interchange ensued. It looked like a playground fight among two kids at recess.

Honestly, I don't remember the total conversation, but I do remember how she 'ate me alive' with her clear articulation of Jehovah Witness doctrine. I fumbled trying to make what I believed make sense. Nothing I said seemed to have any substance. I was embarrassed and deflated. Dejected, I simply walked away saying, "I know whom I believe" (2Timothy 1:12). I felt like a failure.

"... do not worry beforehand, or premeditate what you will speak. But whatever is given you in that hour, speak that; for it is not you who speak, but the Holy Spirit. (Mark 13:11 NKJV)

But the Comforter, which is the Holy Ghost, whom the Father will send in my name, he shall teach you all things, and bring all things to your remembrance, whatsoever I have said unto you. (John 14:26)

The 'go to' scriptures I had recently learned didn't seem to help me. I didn't premeditate on my response, and it appeared as though the Holy Spirit didn't remind me of anything. Instead, He showed me that I needed a firm foundation in the Word of God. Good sermons motivated me, and religious clichés were applauded among my peers; but in real world conflicts, neither were any substitute for the Word of God.

I am thankful that the Holy Spirit used this as a teaching moment for me. I am also thankful that even in my ignorance He was able to work.

A few months later, another coworker who had witnessed the lopsided debate came to me and shared her testimony. She had recently accepted the Lord. She said that during the lunchroom debate she didn't fully understand what I had said. However, there was something about 'how' I said it brought enough conviction that she surrendered her life to Jesus Christ. Believe me, I know this outcome was the work of the Holy Spirit. As I write this, it has been over forty years since all this took place, and she is still serving the Lord today. The Holy Spirit still worked even through my incompetence. As grateful as I was, I still knew this was no excuse for me not to learn more about the Lord.

The Holy Spirit continued to teach me. In the late eighties I became involved in prison ministry. The person in charge of the 'religious services' was a state employee assigned to oversee prisoner activities. She was not a chaplain. She saw what we did as a program for the inmates. If she had any religious affiliation or conviction, it didn't show in how she approached her job. Occasionally, she would call a joint meeting of all the 'religious' volunteers to update us on prison protocol and policies. Among those in attendance were Muslims, Jehovah's Witnesses, Buddhists, Roman Catholic and of course, some Christians.

In one of these meetings a pastor requested that the Christian volunteers be allowed to meet separately from the other groups. His request created some tension in the room. The other religious volunteers interpreted his request as elitism. The prison employee overseeing the volunteers saw it as creating more work for her. I sat there knowing that our beliefs were different, but I did not know enough to confidently defend them.

In one particular meeting I sat next to a Muslim gentleman. During one of our breaks, I questioned him about his beliefs. He shared with me the five pillars of Islam that are mandatory for Muslim life. He was quite confident. I realized that if someone had asked me about what I believed, it would have been difficult for me to articulate it as succinctly as he had described his faith.

This became another teaching moment. As I look back, I realized that I firmly believed in Jesus, but my understanding was still superficial. I knew the Romans Road, and I had a ton of scriptures that would let 'sinners' know how bad off they were. I was 'rapture ready' but lacking in spiritual depth. I was church confident, but superficial in the knowledge of Christ.

Let me be clear. What I am sharing is the path the Lord used to teach me. This is what it took for Him to lay a foundation for what I am doing today. These two episodes were critical to my spiritual development. They were among many other life events that are unique to me. I trust the Holy Spirit will lead you in a path that will reveal God's Son to you in an undeniable way. I want all believers to have the secure revelation that Jesus is the Christ, Son of the Living God.

ONCE AGAIN – ANOTHER JESUS

The apostle Paul challenged the Corinthian believers not to be deceived by those who came preaching 'another Jesus' (2Corinthians 11:3-4). This makes it clear that there are varying versions of Jesus. These variations have the potential of drawing believers away from the faith. To the Galatians, Paul warned them that they should consider those who preach another gospel accursed (Galatians 1:6-9).

It may be difficult to admit, but even our denominational portrayal of Jesus Christ can taint our understanding of who He really is. It is imperative that Jesus as revealed in scripture be understood.

JESUS ACCORDING TO SCRIPTURE

Let's return to my conversation with the Muslim at the prison. Remember, he shared five key things that they believe and do. As I studied the Word of God, the Holy Spirit showed me five key areas that point to Jesus Christ. They became the foundation I needed to understand Jesus Christ as He is revealed in scripture.

I believe these five factors will strengthen your faith. They are important to build your confidence in our Lord and Savior, Jesus Christ. They are not intellectual points to argue with other religions. They are for you. You should learn them. You should know them. It is more important that you demonstrate the power of the risen Lord, than it is to argue over his deity (1Corinthians 2:1-5). As you learn more about Him, you will be positioned to walk in a greater revelation of Jesus Christ.

THE FIVE KEY FACTORS OF THE LORD'S DEITY

What are these five factors? They are (1) His virgin birth, (2) His sinless life, (3) His vicarious death, (4) His bodily resurrection, and (5) His bodily return. All five are necessary to identify the Jesus of scripture. If any one of these are removed or changed, it exposes a religion that rejects Jesus Christ as Lord.

The following is a summary of these five factors. The scope of this book cannot cover them fully. I pray the basic information I share will prompt you to research these in more detail.[1]

THE VIRGIN BIRTH

Therefore the Lord himself shall give you a sign; Behold, a virgin shall conceive, and bear a son, and shall call his name Immanuel. (Isaiah 7:14)

Behold, a virgin shall be with child, and shall bring forth a son, and they shall call his name Emmanuel, which being interpreted is, God with us. (Matthew 1:23)

The entrance of Jesus Christ into the world is the first primary factor relating to His deity. Believers accept that Mary gave birth to Him as a virgin. Why is this important to our faith? Because His prophetic name implied His purpose. Isaiah wrote that His name would be Immanuel. Matthew made sure we knew the meaning of Emmanuel, which is, God with us. This is the reason the virgin birth was necessary. A Holy God became lower than the angels to dwell among His people, to redeem them from the grip of death (Romans 8:3; Hebrews 2:14). Scripture declares that Jesus was God manifest in the flesh (John 1:1, 14; 1Timothy 3:16).

From the beginning, God wanted to dwell with mankind as they managed and ruled the earth (Genesis 1:26-28; Leviticus 26:11-12).

---

[1] For more teaching on this subject, visit The Ekklesia Center YouTube Channel and watch the series, EKKLESIA: ADDRESSING ACCUSATIONS OF BEING A CULT. The five factors relating to the deity of Jesus Christ is taught in greater detail.

Even at the end of the ages, scripture says the heavenly Jerusalem would come down to earth. The result would be that the Tabernacle of God would be with men; and He would be their God and they would be His people. This has always been the divine intent. (Revelation 21:3-4).

In recent years there has been an effort by some to discredit the Virgin Birth. Some say that the story of a child being born from a virgin is a copycat religious tale. They claim that Christianity plagiarized the Virgin Birth from religions that pre-existed Jesus Christ by thousands of years. These distractors seek to place Jesus in the same category as mythological and pagan gods. This has become fodder to bolster antichristian beliefs.

Our faith is founded on the life, death, burial and resurrection of Jesus Christ. When you examine the gods Jesus was allegedly compared to and copied from, you find they are woefully inadequate. Those trying to bring the virgin birth into question, use bits and pieces of mythology that they consider to be false, and compare them with similar factors surrounding the virgin birth. This is done to imply that because mythological and pagan stories are false, then the virgin birth of Jesus is equally false.

The litmus test for believers is evidence. Bits and pieces of similarities pulled from mythology or paganism do not disprove the virgin birth of Christ. The historical, sociological, psychological and of course, biblical evidence that accompany the life of

Christ weaken all attempts to discredit Him. If the devil can discredit His birth, then he can also discredit His life.

Joseph, who was espoused to Mary would have been within his legal rights to divorce her (Deuteronomy 24:1). But he was visited by an angel who encouraged him not to fear taking Mary as his wife – specifically because she was pregnant by the Holy Ghost (Matthew 1:19). This was no small deal. To the casual observer, it appeared as though Mary had been unfaithful to Joseph. His decision not to divorce her would no doubt attract criticism, ridicule and even embarrassment. It was a bold act for him. His response to this matter, based on an angelic visitation, bolsters the fact that Jesus was born as a result of a divine decision.

The Pharisees and Sadducees did not believe Jesus was born of a virgin. They clearly realized that Joseph was not His biological father. They also saw Mary as having been unfaithful to him. Years later this stigma was still being attached to Jesus. It was during a discussion of fatherhood, that the religious leaders tried to publicly embarrass Jesus by saying He was born as a result of fornication (John 8:41). They had no other explanation for Jesus' birth other than human presuppositions of infidelity. In their effort to embarrass and discredit Jesus, they inadvertently revealed that the factors surrounding Jesus birth was unusual, even if they did not recognize it as being divine.

If we deny or ignore the virgin birth, we will be like the Pharisees and Sadducees of the first century. If we disregard the virgin birth, we become blinded to the full essence of Jesus Christ. God became man. Deity and humanity came together in the person of Jesus Christ. If you eliminate the virgin birth, you eliminate the purpose and power of His life on earth.

HIS SINLESS LIFE

Without His virgin birth, the sinless life of Jesus Christ would be suspect.

> For we have not an high priest which cannot be touched with the feeling of our infirmities; but was in all points tempted like as we are, yet without sin (Hebrews 4:15)

Adam failed in the Garden. The one thing he was commanded not to do – he did (Genesis 2:17; 3:6). The result was devastating to all mankind (Romans 5:12). Man has proven over and over throughout history that without God, sin is his portion.

Jesus was made in the likeness of sinful flesh (Romans 8:3). This means that He had the same capacity to sin as any of us. The bible is clear that He was tempted like us in every way. He could have lied. He could have cheated. He could have committed fornication. He could have walked in pride. He could have disobeyed God for His own self-interest. You name it, and He could have done it. Jesus, as a man faced circumstances, situations and people that tested His ability to live holy. Yet, nothing He encountered caused Him to sin. Peter wrote that Jesus didn't sin and nothing He said was deceptive (1Peter 2:22; Hebrews 4:15). This is important because His very purpose for coming was to take away our sins. He succeeded because He had no sin in Himself (1John 3:5).

Before going further, you should see how some religions have attempted to undermine our Lord's sinless life. The tactic used to diminish Jesus employs a deceptive redefining of who He is. They do not overtly say He wasn't sinless, but by changing who scripture declares Him to be, they destabilize His redemptive work in the mind of the uninformed. In other words, when you change who He is, you change the effect of what He does. The fulness of the Godhead was in Jesus bodily, and we are complete in Him (Colossians 2:9-10).

The Jehovah's Witness describe Jesus as a created angel. This teaching takes away His co-equality with God.

> Therefore the Jews sought the more to kill him, because he not only had broken the sabbath, but said also that God was his Father, making himself equal with God. (John 5:18)

> Who, being in the form of God, thought it not robbery to be equal with God
>
> (Philippians 2:6).

The full essence of God was in Jesus Christ. God, not an angel became a man (Hebrews 1:8-14). Jesus was God manifest in the flesh (1Timothy 3:16). Scripture makes it clear that angelic beings are different from human beings (1Corinthians 15:39-40). Therefore, if He was a created angel that became flesh, that eliminates a

Savior who can be touched with the feeling of our infirmities (Hebrews 4:15).

Islam acknowledges the historical life of Jesus. To them, He was just one of many prophets of Allah. They do not believe He had any divine attributes nor was He part of the Godhead. Ironically, some Muslim traditions say that He was sinless, but they do not believe He atoned for any of our sins. Their views regarding Jesus death vary. Generally, they do not believe He died for our sins on the cross. To the Muslim, sin and subsequently salvation, involve both works and fate. To escape the judgment of Allah, the Five Pillars of Islam must be fulfilled.

The Muslim view of Jesus makes Him void of any capacity to redeem us. Even when they accept that He was sinless, there was no purpose for it, and we remain in our sins at the mercy of Allah.

The Jesus of the Mormons is not the Jesus of scripture. The Unity School of Christianity describes Christ as being the name of a super-mind, and Jesus as the name of personal consciousness. I could list many other religions whose beliefs conflict with scripture. The point I want to make is that when you eliminate the reality of Christ being sinless by redefining His person, you also eliminate the purpose for His life[2].

---

[2] Recommended study resource, THE KINGDOM OF THE CULTS by Walter Martin ©1965,1977,1985 Bethany House Publishers

For he hath made him to be sin for us, who knew no sin; that we might be made the righteousness of God in him (2Corinthians 5:21)

Christ hath redeemed us from the curse of the law, being made a curse for us: for it is written, Cursed is every one that hangeth on a tree: (Galatians 3:13)

And ye know that he was manifested to take away our sins; and in him is no sin (1John 3:5)

HIS VICARIOUS DEATH

Philippians 2:8 is interesting to me. Jesus was obedient and submitted Himself to death. I will discuss that point shortly. What makes this verse unique was the emphasis on the type of death He submitted to – death on the cross. To specify the type of death suggests something inimitable about dying in this manner.

The cross has been a stumbling block for many people. It was a cruel, torturous, and unimaginable way to be executed. First century Jews considered anyone who died on a cross to be eternally cursed (Galatians 3:13). There are different views as to whether the cross was shaped like a 'T', or if it was two poles protruding from the ground in the shape of an 'X'. Some described it as just a simple stake; but everyone agrees that the people viewed the cross as a place of death for the worst of criminals. This is the method of death Jesus willfully submitted Himself to.

As the Father knoweth me, even so know I the Father: and I lay down my life for the sheep. And other sheep I have, which are not of this fold: them also I must bring, and they shall hear my voice; and there shall be one fold, and one shepherd. Therefore doth my Father love me, because I lay down my life, that I might take it again. No man taketh it from me, but I lay it down of myself. I have power to lay it down, and I have power to take it again. This commandment have I received of my Father. (John 10:15-18)

Scripture declares that Jesus became sin for us. He was sinless, but He took on sin to die in our place. This mystery has baffled non-believers for centuries. First, *how* could someone take on another person's sin? and second, *why* would someone take on another person's sin?

In the first century, the cross was not celebrated. In time, the symbol of the cross has become a relic of superstition in some religions. Today it is often a piece of jewelry. Sadly, many people have no clue of its significance.

For the preaching of the cross is to them that perish foolishness; but unto us which are saved it is the power of God. (1Corinthians 1:18)

We have summarized the Virgin Birth, the sinless life, and touched a surface explanation of the vicarious death of Jesus. In the next chapter we will review the resurrection. The resurrection is pivotal to our ability to see Jesus as the Christ, Son of the Living God.

6 | The Bodily Resurrection

Jesus is alive. He is the [Living] Christ, Son of the Living God. This chapter is written primarily to reveal the factors relating to the resurrection of Jesus Christ. All of Christianity rises and falls on this one fact. If there was no resurrection, then what we believe is in vain (1Corinthians 15:13-23).

Proof of the resurrection had to be both biblical and secular. There had to be clear historical evidence available to all who made the claim in the first century, but also for us who hold fast to this today. What evidence is there?

PROOF OF DEATH

To make the claim of a bodily resurrection, there had to be proof that Jesus was dead. Because Passover was approaching, the Jews requested that the legs of the men on the crosses were broken, and their bodies be taken down. Of course, this would ensure that if the victim was still alive, escape would be nearly impossible. The legs of the two men who were crucified with Jesus were broken first. When the soldiers came to Jesus, it was obvious that He was already dead. Rather than break the bones in His legs, one of the soldiers thrust a spear in Jesus' side and out came blood and water. I am sure that this unknown soldier had no clue that he was documenting the physical death of Jesus, not only at that time, but throughout all history (John 19:31-34).

THE ART OF CRUCIFIXION

In the last chapter I skimmed the surface of the vicarious death. The fact that Jesus submitted to death on the cross is important. This type of death helps us lay a foundation for the resurrection.

The soldiers who were skilled in the gruesome art of crucifixion, knew when a person was dead. Crucifixion was a long slow death. Breaking the legs of the two thieves before removing their bodies from the cross suggests that there was some evidence of life in them. The very fact that the soldiers did not break Jesus' legs indicates that they clearly knew He was dead. Scripture records that Pilate was surprised that Jesus was already dead when Joseph of Arimathea requested His body (Mark 15:44). The blood and water that spewed out of the body of Jesus is further evidence that He was dead.

Modern forensic scientists have studied the conditions that would cause blood and a watery substance to come out of a dead body. They have concluded that because of the horrendous beating Jesus endured, and the tremendous loss of blood, He would have gone into hypovolemic shock. This condition causes fluid to gather in the sack around the heart and lungs. When the soldier pierced Jesus' side, he undoubtedly forced the spear through Jesus lungs and into His heart releasing the fluid and blood that had accumulated.[1] This becomes modern documentation of Jesus physical death on the cross.

JESUS WAS BURIED

The next thing that took place was the burial of Jesus Christ. It was the dead body of our Lord, wrapped in linen and one hundred pounds of spices and myrrh that was laid in a borrowed tomb (John 19:38-40). This becomes another significant marker in documenting the resurrection.

The Pharisees took precaution to preempt Jesus' claim of resurrection. They requested and received a military watch to guard the tomb. This included not less than four, but potentially as many as thirty soldiers who were to protect the tomb. They were under

---

[1] See https://www.gotquestions.org/blood-water-Jesus.html

the penalty of death if anything happened to the body of Jesus. On the third day, something took place at the tomb. Whether you believe in the resurrection or not, whatever took place resulted in the body of Jesus no longer being found in the tomb. It is the reaction of the soldiers that document this fact.

Of course, I believe what took place was the promised resurrection of Jesus Christ (Matthew 16:21; Mark 9:31). The soldiers fell helplessly to the ground; and Jesus rose from the dead and left the tomb (Matthew 28:4).

What the soldiers did after they realized the body of Jesus was gone becomes another marker in documenting the death, burial and resurrection of the Lord. They immediately knew their fate and went to the Chief Priests for help. It was there that the story was concocted that the disciples came and stole the body while the guards were asleep. This lie exposes another piece of documentation.

If the soldiers had in fact been asleep, this would have been cause for their execution. They needed the influence of the religious leaders to protect them. This lie also wants you to believe that the disciples, who had fled in fear when Jesus was arrested, suddenly had enough courage to sneak past the soldiers to steal the body. This meant they would have to silently break the seal over the tomb. Based on the estimated size, weight and configuration of the stone that covered the mouth of the tomb, it would have required several men to silently roll the stone away[2]. In other words, stealing the body was a logistical impossibility.

What if the disciples had attempted to steal the body? What if they had been caught by the soldiers and a fracas had ensued? The enemies of Jesus would love to have included this in the history books. Imagine how the story of the unskilled disciples fighting against the highly trained soldiers would have played out. It would have been highly probable that several soldiers or even the disciples would have died in such a fight.

Without divine intervention, the disciples would have suffered a devastating defeat. Believers would have loved to have recorded such a victory at the tomb. But if that had happened, it would greatly diminish the reality of the resurrection. If the disciples could have successfully stolen the body of Jesus, it would make the reported resurrection suspect, as the missing body would have been the result of human intervention.

If the disciples had tried to steal the body, most likely, they would have been soundly defeated by the soldiers. All the claims of a resurrection would have been squashed. But history records no such battle ever taking place. The reality was that the disciples were huddled in an upper room in fear (John 20:19).

To prove the resurrection, Jesus' death had to be documented. His bones weren't broken (Psalms 34:20; John 19:36). This sug-

---

[2] Historians estimate the stone could have weighed as much as one to two thousand pounds.

gests the soldiers knew that He was dead. After being stabbed in the side, blood and water poured out of His body, a condition caused by hypovolemic shock. This too became a piece of historical documentation of His death.

It is important to know the strict burial ritual that was observed. The way the body was wrapped, would have made it impossible for Jesus to have escaped from the tomb unassisted. It is important to know the massive stone that covered the tombs entrance, and the fact that it was sealed by the Roman government. It is important to know the fate awaiting the soldiers for 'losing' the body. It is important to know that the disciples were hiding in fear during this entire episode.

Combined, these historical facts point to a cataclysmic event that can only be explained by some supernatural intervention. Simply put, Jesus was buried and rose from the dead.

JESUS' PROGRESSIVE APPEARANCES

Jesus first appeared to Mary Magdalene and Mary, the mother of James and Joses (Matthew 27:56; 28:1). They had been to the tomb and instructed by an angel to go tell the disciples He was risen from the dead. As they were quickly going, Jesus appeared to them. Their response indicated that they clearly recognized who He was (Matthew 28:7-10). Jesus told the women to tell the disciples to meet Him in Galilee. This now gets more interesting.

Then the eleven disciples went away into Galilee, into a mountain where Jesus had appointed them. And when they saw him, they worshipped him: but some doubted. (Matthew 28:16-17)

The eleven surviving disciples met the Living Lord face to face in Galilee. Some of them worshipped Him; but it is remarkable that some doubted. Yes, some of the men who had spent nearly three years with Jesus, now doubted His presence before them.

Reading through the Gospels, it becomes clear that more proof had to be provided to the disciples. Jesus scolded them for not believing the report of the women. He had to settle them down after they panicked, assuming He was a spirit. He had them touch the wounds in His hands and feet, declaring He was not a spirit, but flesh and bone. Jesus even took time to eat a meal before them (Mark 16:14; Luke 24:36-43).

Thomas, who had missed the other appearances of Jesus was the last holdout. He made it clear that he would not believe unless he personally touched the scars in Jesus' hands and put his hand in the wound in His side. That is exactly what Jesus allowed Thomas to do (John 20:24-28).

MORE PROOF...

Luke, who wrote the Gospel bearing His name as well as the Book of Acts, had two significant observations. These are important to us today in our quest to lay a foundation for seeing Jesus as the Christ, Son of the Living God.

WHY TWO MEN COULD NOT SEE

For forty days after His crucifixion, Jesus continued to teach things regarding the Kingdom of Heaven. During this time, He proved over and over that He was literally alive (Acts 1:3). The King James version says He did this with many 'infallible' proofs.

The Greek word for infallible is 'tekmerion'. The idea it portrays is that what has been proven cannot be denied. It means that the evidence regarding a matter is so solid that any and all doubt is eliminated. Paul attested that after the Lord's resurrection, Jesus had been seen alive by over five hundred people. He made a point of saying that many of those who had seen Him were still alive (1Corinthians 15:6). Even after Jesus had ascended back to heaven, Paul claimed to have seen Him too. This no doubt was in reference to his Damascus road experience (Acts 9:17).

One incident of Jesus being seen after His resurrection took place on the road to Emmaus. This event reveals what can keep us from receiving a revelation of Jesus Christ. There are several markers in this story that can help us.

The trip to Emmaus took place on the same day that Peter had verified that the tomb Jesus had been buried in was empty (Luke 24:12-13). As Cleopas and his traveling companion made their way down the road, Jesus joined them and struck up a conversation. He asked them, "What are you talking about, and why are you so sad?"

Cleopas tried to explain what had recently taken place. He assumed that Jesus had to be a stranger in Jerusalem for not being aware of the crucifixion. He went on to share how the high hopes they had were destroyed when Jesus of Nazareth died. Stop! Cleopas and his friend were literally talking with Jesus, but scripture makes a peculiar observation.

...their eyes were holden that they should not know him. (Luke 24:16)

Physically, neither of the two men were blind. But something had obscured their vision making it impossible for them to recognize Jesus. The New English Bible says that something held their eyes from seeing who He was.[3] What was it that prohibited them from seeing Jesus. It is one of the same things that blinds many today – religious presuppositions.

The two men painfully relayed the story of Jesus' crucifixion. They shared what they knew about Him. They had seen Jesus as a prophet who was mighty in deed and word. They were distraught over the fact that Jesus had been condemned by the Chief Priests and crucified. Until that point, they had pinned all their hopes on Him.

---

[3] OXFORD UNIVERSITY PRESS AND CAMBRIDGE UNIVERSITY PRESS. *The New English Bible: New Testament.* Copyright © 1961 by The Delegates of the Oxford University and the Syndics of the Cambridge University press. Reprinted by permission

Then, as if they didn't know how to comprehend what happened next, they spoke of the women who had found the tomb empty. Even some of their own company had verified this fact, but they clearly didn't know what to make of it (Luke 24:18-24). Jesus stopped their bemoaning with an abrupt reproof.

First, He addressed the fact that they did not believe ALL that the prophets had said. This suggests that they didn't know, had overlooked, or misinterpreted key elements of prophetic text. Remember, they only had what we call the Old Testament. They would have read in Isaiah that a Child was born, and a Son was given and may have misinterpreted the government on His shoulders as being the Jewish government overthrowing Roman oppression (Isaiah 9:6; Acts 1:6).

There is no way to definitively determine if they knew that Jesus was the person the prophet said would be wounded for our transgressions, bruised for our iniquities, who would endure the chastisement of our peace, and by His stripes we would be healed (Isaiah 53:4-5). But it is clear by Jesus' words that they had not understood ALL that the prophets had said.

Second, Jesus asked a two-part question that exposed the source of the two men's blindness.

Ought not Christ to have suffered these things, AND to enter into his glory?
(Luke 24:26)

For the two men this query uprooted a long-held belief. How could a person who was crucified be able to enter God's glory? You may not immediately see why this was a problem for them – but here it is.

'If a man has committed a sin deserving of death, and he is put to death, and you hang him on a tree, 'his body shall not remain overnight on the tree, but you shall surely bury him that day, SO THAT YOU DO NOT DEFILE THE LAND WHICH THE LORD YOUR GOD IS GIVING YOU AS AN INHERITANCE; FOR HE WHO IS HANGED IS ACCURSED OF GOD. (Deuteronomy 21:22-23 NKJV)

The law had taught Israel that crucifixion was the worst form of execution. The victim was considered as cursed, not only for the crimes they had committed, but also cursed by God (Galatians 3:13). When Joseph of Arimathea requested the body of Jesus, he could have been motivated by a combination of honor and his understanding of Jewish law. Removing the body and carefully wrapping it in linen and covering it with expensive myrrh and spices was an act of honor. Nicodemus, a ruler of the Jews supplied the burial material (John 19:39). He also was well versed in the Law of Moses.

Could removing the body of Jesus from the cross also have been connected to the Jewish belief that Jerusalem was their land; even though at that time it was under Roman oppression? Remember, they were taught that leaving the body on the tree would cause the land to be defiled. It is easy to conclude that Joseph and

Nicodemus were honoring the Lord and protecting the land at the same time.

In the religious understanding of the two men who met Jesus on the road to Emmaus, crucifixion meant Jesus was cursed of God. This belief made it impossible for them to see Jesus entering into glory.

One of the key factors necessary to see Jesus as the Christ, Son of the Living God, is to allow the Holy Spirit to remove religious blinders from our eyes. Too often our view of Jesus is filtered by our religious presuppositions and traditions. They keep us from seeing Jesus as He is. The evangelical Jesus looks entirely different from the Pentecostal Jesus. The liturgical Jesus is not the same as the non-denominational Jesus.

There are incidents recorded in scripture that carry a ton of symbolism. Such was the conversion of Saul on the road to Damascus. After being confronted by Jesus, Paul was very much like the two men traveling to Emmaus. His eyes were open, but he couldn't see anyone (Acts 9:8). For three days he was completely blind. Ananias cautiously obeyed God to go and see Saul. His mission was to pray for him that his sight would be restored. When he prayed, scales fell from Saul's eyes and his sight was restored (Acts 9:10-20).

Saul was physically blinded. However, before this he was blinded by his deeply held religious beliefs (Galatians 1:13-14; Philippians 3:4-7). This religious blindness made him believe he was justified in persecuting the Lord's ekklesia (Acts 9:1-2; 1Timothy 1:13). What you need to understand is that your religious beliefs can obscure your sight. As a result, what you see, or don't see will drive your actions.

Religion can taint how we see Jesus Christ and interact with other believers. There are certain denominations that teach the gifts of the Holy Spirit (speaking in tongues, healing, and prophecy), were limited to the first century. This belief limits their ability to trust God for supernatural acts today. Other denominations rely heavily on the outward manifestation of the Spirit. They often equate emotional outburst as the presence of the Holy Spirit. For them, quiet, meditative worship is considered weak Christianity. These are extreme examples, but take note of your response to what you just read. Your inner reaction may give you an indication of your own filters.

> But the natural man receiveth not the things of the Spirit of God: for they are foolishness unto him: neither can he know them, because they are spiritually discerned. (1Corinthians 2:14)

Religious beliefs create most of the spiritual blindness in believers. Religious beliefs create an aura of correctness. Religious systems often will surround itself with scriptures that are cut and pasted together to validate itself. The dilemma with spiritual blindness is that an individual cannot see it in their own life.

In 1992, the Lord made it clear that He had called me to the work that has evolved into what I do today. He said that the vision I see was His. Then He said something that still resonates in my spirit. He said, "My hands are hampered by disobedience and religion in you." I could not ignore the connection He made between disobedience and religion.

Religion deadens hearing. Several times in scripture we read if any have ears to hear, let him hear (Matthew 13:9; Mark 4:23). In other places people are said to be dull of hearing (Acts 28:27; Hebrews 5:11). In neither case are these people physically deaf, but rather unable to comprehend what is before them.

Disobedience is caused when we elevate our religious belief above God's instructions. Just as Paul threatened and persecuted the ekklesia, we too assume that our long-held, and misguided beliefs are Godly. Remember, at the time Paul was persecuting the ekklesia, he felt he was upholding his Judaic heritage (Acts 8:1; 9:1-2). In his mind, he did not think he was doing anything wrong. Our actions reveal what we believe.

The Lord helped me to see that 'hearing through religious filters' hampers His ability to work in my life. My 'tradition' has the effect of nullifying the Word of God (Matthew 15:6). When I elevate my tradition above the Word of God, I position my will against His, and I am sure you know who will lose that battle. Daily I am learning how to submit my will to His – even when I don't fully comprehend all the pieces. Comprehension is not a prerequisite to obedience.

To receive the revelation that Jesus is the Christ, Son of the Living God, we must repent of any preconceived filters that obscure our sight and hearing. Our traditions and denominational beliefs must be laid at the foot of the cross. Only then can we be positioned to see Him as He is (1John 3:2). Let's look at other blinders that keep us from seeing Jesus Christ, as well as other filters that can dampen our hearing of the truth.

7 | Culture, Ideology and Race

Do you really desire to know Jesus as the Christ, Son of the Living God? If so, prepare to lay aside every weight and the sin that so easily can throw you off course (Hebrews 12:1).

In his letter to the Ephesians, Paul's desire was that God would give them the spirit of revelation in the knowledge of Jesus Christ.

> *[I cease] not to give thanks for you, making mention of you in my prayers; THAT THE GOD OF OUR LORD JESUS CHRIST, THE FATHER OF GLORY, MAY GIVE UN-TO YOU THE SPIRIT OF WISDOM AND REVELATION IN THE KNOWLEDGE OF HIM: The eyes of your understanding being enlightened; that ye may know what is the*

hope of his calling, and what the riches of the glory of his inheritance in the saints, (Ephesians 1:16-18).

Once again, we see that it is God who gives revelation and that revelation is found in knowing His Son.

In one of His final private moments with His disciples, Jesus prayed a powerful prayer. In it, He reaffirmed that everything revolved around knowing God and the one He had sent (John 17:1-3). Peter in his letter to the believers in Rome, reiterated this fact several times. He said grace and peace is multiplied and that we receive all things relating to life and godliness through the knowledge of Jesus Christ (2Peter 1:2-3). After outlining a litany of attributes every believer should pursue, he concluded that with them we would not be barren or unfruitful in the knowledge of Jesus Christ (2Peter 1:5-8). He later ends with the admonition to grow in grace and in the knowledge of our Lord Jesus Christ (2Peter 3:18). One passage I want to bring to your attention is 2Peter 2:20.

> *For if after they have ESCAPED THE POLLUTIONS OF THE WORLD THROUGH THE KNOWLEDGE OF THE LORD AND SAVIOUR JESUS CHRIST, they are again entangled therein, and overcome, the latter end is worse with them than the beginning.*

In the verses preceding this, and those that follow, Peter describes people who had been horribly corrupt, and had come out of debauchery, only to return to it again. After being re-entangled, they sadly ended up in a worse condition than they were before.

This is exactly what Jesus had said could happen (Luke 11:24-26). Although this describes a horrible end, I want you to take note of how they fled in the first place. They had originally *escaped the pollutions of the world through the knowledge of the Lord and Savior Jesus Christ.*

We have discussed in the previous chapter the effect religious presuppositions have in limiting our ability to accurately see the Lord. In this chapter, I want to show you three other pollutants that have the same destructive impact; they are culture, ideology and race.

On the surface, you may not see how these can be serious pollutants. However, any belief, activity, or system that is allowed to rise above the knowledge and purpose of God in Christ is in fact a pollutant in our faith. Any belief that contradicts the values of the Kingdom of God is a pollutant and must be avoided.

> *For though we walk in the flesh, we do not war after the flesh: (For the weapons of our warfare are not carnal, but mighty through God to the pulling down of strong holds;) CASTING DOWN IMAGINATIONS, AND EVERY HIGH THING THAT EXALTETH ITSELF AGAINST THE KNOWLEDGE OF GOD, AND BRINGING INTO CAPTIVITY EVERY THOUGHT TO THE OBEDIENCE OF CHRIST; And having in a readiness to revenge all disobedience, when your obedience is fulfilled. (2Corinthians 10:3-6)*

Our role is to cast down anything that attempts to rise above the knowledge of God in Christ. This chapter will help to alert you to how culture, ideologies and race can become hindrances to seeing

Jesus as the Christ, Son of the Living God. In this chapter, I will show you more about Jesus Christ. Knowing Him is the only antidote for escape from any pollutant. The more you know about Him, the more apt you are to receive the revelation that He is the Christ, Son of the Living God.

LAYING A KINGDOM FOUNDATION

Immediately after Peter made the declaration Jesus is the Christ, Son of the Living God, Jesus made it clear that it would be the one revelation by which He would build His ekklesia. Jesus immediately declared that the power of that revelation would be powerful enough to defeat the Gates of Hades. It is what Jesus said next that is critical for us today. "I give you the keys of the Kingdom of Heaven..." (Matthew 16:19).

Paul wrote that we are delivered from darkness and translated into the Kingdom of God's Son (Colossians 1:13). The problem is that many drag their cultural, ideological, and racial hang-ups into the Kingdom. This happens because many do not have a clear understanding of the values of the Kingdom.

Before we look deeper into culture, ideology, and race as we know them. I asked Dr. Leonard Robinson, a prolific teacher on the Kingdom of God, to give you an understanding of the culture of the Kingdom. I believe his contribution is important to laying a groundwork for understanding things that pollute our relationship with Jesus Christ.

UNDERSTANDING THE CULTURE OF THE KINGDOM
BY DR. LEONARD ROBINSON

The Kingdom of God according to Old and New Testament scripture is the royal rule, order, and active reign of God over a people and over a territory, impacting them with His will. It produces a culture of citizens who exercise dominion over life's circumstances with the presence of God working with them as power, might, dominion and wisdom over every strategy of the enemy.

This definition of the Kingdom stems from the Greek word "Basileia" and the Hebrew words "Radah" and "Malkuth" or "Mamlakah". All these words denote dominion and rule or to reign. When applied to God, it means that He rules or reigns over a people who submit to His commandments. These people would rule as Adam was to rule over the earth. Through the new birth man can again reign with Christ in life as we submit to the commandments of Jesus, which are the commandments of God for a people He has chosen for Himself (Romans 5:17; Genesis 1:26-28).

The culture of the Kingdom can be viewed as the fruit of the Spirit made manifest through those who yield and submit themselves to the Holy Spirit and the mysteries of the Kingdom found in the Word of God. It is the character of Christ made manifest through the followers of Jesus who acknowledge His lordship over and through their lives (Galatians 5:22).

Jesus hinges entrance into the eternal Kingdom on obedience to the commandments of the Father (Matthew 7:21). More than the eschatological view of the return of Christ (pretribulation or post tribulation theories), it remains that Jesus alone describes how anyone will enter into the eternal Kingdom. Consequently, what we see is that as much as it is important to be Born again, it is also important to reflect a life of spiritual maturity resulting from being submitted to the commandments of God the Father.

According to Jesus, the Father is as interested in the culture and the maturity of the children as He is in them being Born Again. The Father is looking for culture. Another word for culture is character. The importance of Kingdom culture cannot be understated. The culture of the Kingdom is the character of Christ as revealed by the fruit of the Spirit. The culture of the Kingdom is made manifest in everyone who submits to the Holy Spirit and the Word of God.

According to The Miriam Webster Dictionary, culture is defined as the customary beliefs, social forms, and material traits of a racial, religious, or social group. Further defined as the characteristic features of everyday existence (such as diversions or a way of life) shared by people in a place or time.

From a Kingdom perspective, culture is identified by the actions of a group of people. It is a part of a tribe or sect of people who are members of a tribe, or group, who all live in a particular geography and whose practices, rituals and customs are uniquely identified as being a part of that group's beliefs, which may include certain customs, rituals and traditions.

Acts 11:19-30 reveals that the followers of Jesus "were called Christians at Antioch." The reason is that they were a band of people who followed Jesus' teachings by keeping His commandments. These disciples, as children of God and citizens of the Kingdom, were marked by their obedience. They loved one another and lived holy and separate from the world. They had become a community that had all things in common, taking care of one another and breaking bread together daily. These followers of Jesus met daily and prayed, fasted, and served one another as Jesus had commanded.

The first century believers were identified as Christians because they were living the culture that was identifiable by others. The fruit of the Spirit can be seen in those who submit to the Word of God and yield to the commandments of Jesus and the Holy Spirit. In other words, without submission to the commandments of Jesus, and the Holy Spirit, you cannot arrive at the culture of the Kingdom.

Many people today who profess salvation through Jesus Christ never progress into the maturity that identifies them as Christians. Without renewing their mind to the will of God, by the Word of God, and submitting to the Holy Spirit, they cannot produce or in any way manifest the fruit of the Spirit. Carnal mindedness is fleshly or sensory ruled thinking which manifest itself in a character, a lifestyle, and a culture contrary to the life that the Father has purposed for His children.

The Merriam Webster Dictionary further describes culture as 'the integrated pattern of human knowledge, belief, and behavior that depends on the capacity for learning and transmitting knowledge to succeeding generations.' Culture also denotes to grow in a prepared medium (such as the microorganisms associated with yogurt).

Culture among the saints is the growth that is supposed to take place within the assembly of saints who obtain the knowledge of the Kingdom of God/the Kingdom of Heaven. It is by application of the principles and precepts of the Kingdom as revealed in the word of God. It is the teachings of Jesus as foundational; and, by the ministry of the apostles, prophets, evangelists, pastors and teachers, to mature saints into the stature of Christ. In other words, the culture of [the ekklesia] is to be the character of Christ. When people see this culture, they see Christ. As saints, we possess the Kingdom under the heavens.

We reflect the culture of the Kingdom (Daniel 7:18-27).

CULTURAL POLLUTANTS

As you can see from Dr. Robinson's outline, culture is deep and multifaceted. We toss around phrases like American culture, African culture, Middle Eastern culture, European Culture, French Culture or Asian Culture and our minds default to a stereotypical image of what that culture looks like.

There are many social cultures that exists. They are found in corporate environments, school settings, and within religious groups. It is the latter that we will explore in this chapter. Therefore, knowledge of the culture of the Kingdom is important. By understanding Kingdom culture, it becomes easier to recognize when human cultures conflict with the purposes of God.

CULTURE TODAY

Dr. Robinson shows us that in our obedience to Jesus Christ, we reflect the Kingdom of God. We look like Christ whose character is revealed in the culture of the Kingdom. In essence, we look, sound, and act like citizens from another country.

The language and social interactions within a culture become deeply engrained. Language is not limited to the native tongue of a people group but also includes the *way* things are said. Inter-cultural words and phrases are spoken that make sense to those within the culture but may be confusing to an outsider.

What does this have to do with knowing Jesus as the Christ, Son of the Living God? Our culture often molds our view of the Lord. Our doctrines are at times created and interpreted by our culture. Instead of seeing Jesus 'as He is', we view Him 'as our religious culture defines or describes Him'. In one culture Jesus is a loving and gracious Savior, while in another He saves you but then watches over a never-ending list of do's and don'ts and any infraction would be met with potentially eternal consequences.

You may not realize it, but even as you read this book your cultural views of scripture weigh in on how you accept or reject what you are reading. You may see this as elementary information and miss the greater point of this book altogether.

There is neither Jew nor Greek, there is neither bond nor free, there is neither male nor female: for ye are all one in Christ Jesus. (Galatians 3:28)

This passage is often quoted to validate our oneness in Christ Jesus. Yet many times the distinctions Paul listed are obscured or glossed over. Yes, in the eyes of the Lord, we are all one in Christ Jesus, but Paul wasn't suggesting that a Jew suddenly became a Greek as a result of their oneness in Christ. He wasn't implying that the bond slave would now have the earthly status of the free man because they were in Christ. He most definitely wasn't implying that a male would become a female, or vice-versa as a result of their oneness in Christ. Paul was saying, that regardless of these distinctions, we are one in spirit in Christ Jesus.

In his letter to the Galatians, Paul was confronting the confusion that ensued after some from Jerusalem had tried to impose circumcision on them (Acts 15:1; Galatians 5:2). The Gentiles, specifically the Galatians Paul was addressing, had no historical context or understanding of circumcision. Scripture makes it clear that the Jews who wanted to impose circumcision on the Gentiles, were believers (Acts 15:5). I would suggest that they were not malicious, but rather set in their cultural ways that had been established in them through years of religious programming. They believed that to be saved, the Galatians would have to assimilate into the Judaic culture and belief system. They had elevated their cultural heritage over the core principle of accepting Christ.

Culture is not necessarily a bad thing. It reflects the environment that nurtured us into who we are. This is typified in the definition of culture where organisms are grown in a prepared medium, specifically known as a petri dish. The norms of our culture drive many of the expectations we have in life. Our culture becomes the atmosphere where our values find validity. It is the 'way of life' for people groups. How people interact with each other in a culture is generally understood without explanation. It falls under the adage, "...it goes without being said." The problem arises when our cultural expectations, beliefs and values override the Word of God.

Cultural blinders evolve over time. They become unwritten social laws. At some point those within a culture begin to believe their ways are the norm for everyone.

Some time ago I attended a funeral that was held at a very liturgical ministry. The officiant led one ritual after another that was interspersed with short scriptural readings and brief comments about the deceased. As we were leaving the service, one person who had accompanied me asked, "Were these people saved?" Nothing the person had seen lined up with that person's cultural experience relating to funerals. There were no choirs or lengthy testimonies about the deceased. There was very little outward emotional expression. And to cap it off, the minister did not preach what this person considered to be a soul-stirring message. In the mind of my acquaintance, this suggested a lack of salvation. To be clear, my acquaintance was not questioning the salvation of the deceased, but rather that of the officiant and members of that ministry.

As simple as this example may appear, this actually reflects a common mindset among many. Salvation is linked to how we express it in our culture. The petri dish of our culture drives what we often come to believe. I do not advocate the rejection of our respective cultures. God did not give us our uniqueness to be buried. Each of us are part of a divine mosaic that blends together to express the fulness of Christ.

The problems arise when we elevate our culture as superior to another. More problems arise when our cultural beliefs conflict with the Word of God. Cultures that worship other gods are not included in the purposes or protection of God (Exodus 20:3; 34:14). Ultimately, as long as our earthly cultures are elevated, they can potentially pollute our ability to receive the revelation of Jesus Christ being the Son of the Living God. Let's turn our attention to the other two pollutants that can distort our view of the Lord: ideology and race.

IDEOLOGY

Ideology is defined as a system of ideas and ideals, especially one which forms the basis of economic or political theory and policy.

Most of us are aware of the problems facing this world. You can't turn on your television without being hit with a barrage of conflicts, wars, political fighting, racial and ethnic conflicts, and so much more.

Abortion, gun violence, same-sex marriages and the like are in our faces, in our communities, in our families, and in our nation.

What has been the response of the current church system? To address some of the ills of society, some have embraced humanistic social ideologies. They become more concerned with relevance than righteousness. They seek to be accepted in society. This has resulted in many 'churches' adopting ideological beliefs that coincide more with humanism rather than Kingdom thinking. In their quest for relevance, they have embraced practices and policies that are an antithesis to the Word of God.

Some religious groups are unable to see Jesus as He is, because the Jesus of scripture conflicts with the Jesus of their ideology. They defend their ideology more than they stand for Christ. This becomes a filter that prohibits many from seeing Jesus as He is.

RACE AND ETHNICITY

It saddens me that race has distorted the sight of many professing Christians. Some have used the bible to perpetuate racial division, to support the evils of slavery, and to pit one race against another.

This problem goes from one extreme to another. On one side there are those who claim they do not see color. This line of thought inadvertently undermines the creativity of God to create man in many skin hues. The other extreme is those who teach that God's desire is to keep the races separate and that somehow mixing races is some form of sin. Added to this are the many discussions relating to Jesus' race. The pendulum swings from one end to the other. The image of the 'white' Jesus that has dominated Christianity in the west is being challenged by those who state Jesus was a man of color. As a black man, I have had to face those who believe that Christianity is "the white man's" religion. It is not easy being accused of being insensitive to your own race.

With all this as a backdrop, I want to be clear that your race and my race cannot be overlooked, but in no case should race be elevated above the knowledge of Jesus Christ. No one reading this book chose their race. It was gifted to you at birth. To use it as a tool of superiority or to ignore the glory of another race shows both ignorance and is a denial of the wisdom of our creator.

Aaron and Miriam pretended to question whether God only spoke to Moses. The reality was that they had an issue with Moses because he had married an Ethiopian woman. It's intriguing to me that this resulted in Miriam experiencing a bout of leprosy. Not once during this episode did God make excuses for who Moses had married – that was clearly a dysfunction lurking in the hearts of Aaron and Miriam (Numbers 12).

It was Peter, a Jew, who first declared that Jesus is the Christ, Son of the Living God. Yet, the Lord had to deal with some latent bigotry in his heart. While praying on the roof, Peter received a vision to eat from a palate of animals that the Jews considered unclean. This led to him going to the home of Cornelius, specifically identified as an Italian. It was there that God showed Peter that 'He is no respecter of persons, but in every nation, the man who has fear of Him and does righteousness is pleasing to Him' (Acts 10:34-35). Unfortunately, Peter struggled with this for some time as Paul had to confront him regarding this same issue in Antioch (Galatians 2:11-13).

The Twentieth Century New Testament records Paul telling those in Athens that God "made all races of the earth's surface from one blood" (Acts 17:26). The racial friction we experience today is a direct result of fallen man tampering with God's design for humanity.

> *If a man says, I have love for God, and has hate for his brother, his words are false: for how is the man who has no love for his brother whom he has seen, able to have love for God whom he has not seen? And this is the word which we have from him, that he who has love for God is to have the same love for his brother. (1John 4:20-21 Bible in Basic English)*

To receive the revelation that Jesus is the Christ, Son of the Living God means that our racial views must be laid at the foot of the cross. This does not mean that we ignore race. Racial conflicts are birthed from the gates of hades. As people who represent the Kingdom of Heaven, we must seek ways to undo the damage that has been done by racial injustices. It will require repentance, forgiveness, and intentional acts of justice.

I have previously discussed religion, culture, and ideology as barriers to grasping the full revelation of Jesus Christ. The issue of race adds its own idiosyncrasies to these humanistic filters. Our goal is to preserve our racial and ethnic heritage in a manner that pleases our Lord.

If we refuse to allow our cultural, ideological and racial realities to be filters in our understanding of the culture of the Kingdom, our ability to see Jesus as the Christ, Son of the Living God is greatly enhanced.

8 | Religion or Revelation

Many well-meaning believers have only a cerebral understanding of Jesus Christ. They fall short of having the revelation that He is the Christ, Son of the Living God. They have been 'in church' long enough to know the spiritual lingo and how to conduct themselves around other believers. The problem is that they become spiritually sterilized, not consciously expecting any real results from their faith walk.

Religion has a unique way of 'dumbing down' our relationship with the Lord. We fall into the trap of the weekly 'go to church' ritual. The music and the message are good for the moment. There is an emotional euphoria that creates a soulish motivation to do something better. That feeling may last a few days after the service, but often by the end of the week we are back to our old ways. The lack of discipling, combined with low expectations result in a Christian populace who survive on spiritual clichés and routine methodologies.

It is in the planning

If you think I am over generalizing, I suggest that most church leadership often spends more time preparing for the Sunday presentation, rather than the care of those who come to see it. I recently heard an interview with a prominent pastor of a mega-church who admitted that much of his bible study had been spent preparing for messages. He spent very little time studying and re-flecting on the Word of God for personal edification. Thankfully he realized this flaw and is correcting this pattern in his life.

What about making disciples? Jesus instructed us to make dis-ciples of nations (Matthew 28:19). Paul said to present what he taught to faithful men who will teach others (2Timothy 2:2). There are more than fifty scriptures in the New Testament that speak di-rectly to our interaction with other believers. The common church structure does not give way to the personal interaction required to make disciples of the Lord.

Our discipling efforts have been reduced to a series of classes concluding with a certificate. In effect, new believers are taught how to function within the church system, but very little about navigating through life. That is why we see those who can serve admirably within the local church but fail miserably with their family, their finances and emotional well-being.

The Sunday services are orchestrated to garner the greatest emotional response possible. Yes, I know we outwardly claim our intent is to win souls to the Lord, but the unspoken motive is to grow our church. Church size has become the barometer that determines how successful we are. Christian magazines and the internet are filled with conferences that claim to teach 'How To Attract More First Time Visitors', 'How To Increase Your Church Size', How To Get People To Give More', and the list goes on and on. There is a market for these cut and paste – one size fits all – conferences. However, I would suggest our methodologies of accomplishing these things lack a key ingredient. Let me explain.

IT'S SHOWTIME

Several years ago, I met with the leadership of a growing ministry in our area. They shared with me what they considered to be the secret to their success.

Every Sunday their services consisted of great music from their quasi-professional Praise Team. There was often a short skit presented by their Drama Team, or worship dance that coincided with the Pastor's message for the week. The weekly announcements were professionally shown as mini infomercials on a big screen in their sanctuary. They rivaled what you would see on television. The Pastor would bring a message, often accompanied by elaborate stage props and various sound effects. Special lighting added to the ambience in the room. Scriptures and key comments were shown on the big screen that in effect, replaced the need to have a bible. This all served to draw more and more people to their church. This production required the well-coordinated efforts from the ministry staff to pull this weekly event off. They measured their success by the number of new people who joined them.

Every Monday, the Pastor and the staff would meet to review and critique the Sunday service. They would look for ways to tweak what they had done for the purpose of improving the next service. The Pastor would give a summary of his next message, and each of the departments would go to work creating their part. By the end of the week, all the pieces were finished, and the next Sunday experience was ready to go.

At the time, I saw this as an innovative way to 'do ministry'. I was looking for ways to 'grow' our church and seriously gave thought to using some of their methods. Unfortunately, the innovative image this 'church' portrayed came to an end as it experienced a sad chain of events that nearly destroyed it.

In the years since my meeting with the leadership, this church has gone through some drastic and somewhat painful changes. The Pastor was dismissed for infidelity. Their small groups spent less time in the study of the Word and became known as social gatherings for wine tasting. Some of their Sunday services included people who shared their life journey through body tattoos. In the name of being 'seeker sensitive' they appeared to focus more on carnal desires than spiritual growth. Many people left. Today, they have changed their name, hired a new Pastor, and appear to be moving in a clearer more bible-based direction.

I share this story as it helps to show what lengths some will go to draw people to their church under the guise of winning the lost. Other similar stories include the pastor who did a rodeo ride with a live bull in their Sunday service. Another pastor did a holographic snake to show the story of Moses rod turning into a serpent. Still another pastor exhibited his exotic car on the stage to demonstrate what he claimed to be the power of the Holy Spirit. These antics excited the flesh and maybe drew some to join their churches; but in my opinion did nothing to disciple new believers.

WHAT DO YOU HEAR?

Now is my soul troubled; and what shall I say? Father, save me from this hour: but for this cause came I unto this hour. Father, glorify thy name. Then came there a voice from heaven, saying, I have both glorified it, and will glorify it again. The people therefore, that stood by, and heard it, said that it thundered: others said, An angel spake to him. Jesus answered and said, This voice came not because of me, but for your sakes. Now is the judgment of this world: now shall the prince of this world be cast out. AND I, IF I BE LIFTED UP FROM THE EARTH,

WILL DRAW ALL MEN UNTO ME. THIS HE SAID, SIGNIFYING WHAT DEATH HE SHOULD DIE. (John 12:27-33)

Jesus was beginning to feel somewhat anxious as the time grew closer for Him to die on the cross. Yet, He knew this was His assignment and prayed for the Father to glorify His Name. When the voice from heaven spoke, there were mixed responses from the people standing nearby.

One group said it thundered. This implies that there are people who can be around Jesus, but not close enough to discern what is being said. What they hear is inaudible. To them, there is no distinction in the sound from heaven from the sound of life. As a result, there is no change in their lives.

Others heard the voice and attributed it to an angel. To me this suggests that at times what we hear is filtered through our spirituality which may or may not be accurately aligned with the Father. Jesus clarified what they all heard. He made sure they understood that what they heard was for them, not Him. He let them know that the gauntlet had been thrown down bringing judgment to the world. He went on to declare that satan, the prince of this world, would be cast out. He spoke of being lifted up from the earth which revealed His complete submission to the will of the Father. John, the writer of this text made sure we understood that Jesus was speaking of His death on the cross.

Jesus was first lifted up at Calvary. There, He was lifted up on a cross to die and shed His blood in order to reconcile us back to the Father (Ephesians 2:16; Colossians 1:20). He will not be lifted up on the cross again. It was only required for Him to die one time for our sins (1Peter 3:18). Today we must recognize and acknowledge Him for being lifted up in our behalf. We must continually lift Him up for all the world to see. How do we lift Him up today?

We lift Him up with praise, adoration, extolling and worshiping Him. Yet, this cannot be done without declaring His death, burial and resurrection (1Corinthians 15:1-4). This is often the missing ingredient in our efforts. We have powerful sound and lighting, but we fail to lift up Jesus. Our praise and worship is often reduced to well-orchestrated songfests, but we fail to lift up Jesus. Our sermons stir us emotionally, but often fail to lift up Jesus. God is not moved by these carnal displays (Isaiah 1:10-15). Of course, Jesus is the subject matter, but he is portrayed within the context we design. I realize there is a thin line between our religious rhetoric and truly lifting up Jesus. I have been guilty of blurring this line, and if you are honest, you have too. The proof is in what happens after we worship and after we preach.

First, are people drawn to Christ? He said that if He is lifted up, He would draw all men to Himself. Paul wrote that the gospel is the power of God for salvation (Romans 1:16). Second, once they come to Christ, do we fit them into our church system, or do we commit to the work of making them a disciple of Jesus Christ?

A Word About Making Disciples

What does it mean to make disciples? It is not requiring them to regularly attend church services. Some consider their New Members classes, or discipleship classes as an efficient way to teach more new believers at one time. We should desire effectiveness over efficiency. Discipling is a personal commitment to see that Christ is formed in a new believer (Romans 8:29; Galatians 4:19).

I am not opposed to classroom training. However, classes place all the students in the same category. Classes do not take into consideration the varying needs among the students. Some may be recovering from addictions. Others could be hurting from marital or relationship problems. Some have been deeply wounded emotionally. Discipling demands hands-on close interaction that helps a person navigate towards wholeness in Christ Jesus.

We all have our own unique needs. Jesus healed many people during His ministry. Yet, the need of the paralytic was not the same as that of the blind man (Mark 2:8-12; John 9:1-3). Jesus dealt with the woman at the well, and the woman caught in adultery specific to their individual needs (John 4:1-24; 8:3-11). His ministry to Nicodemus differed from His ministry to the rich young ruler (Luke 18:18-24; John 3:1-15). We must understand that God will use us to minister to the specific and unique needs of the people we encounter.

The line must be drawn between developing new church members and making disciples. Un-discipled new members can perform various roles for the benefit of the church, and still suffer with issues that are hidden from view. They can attend services week after week and still be secretly dabbling in pornography. I have seen 'pastors' leading congregations with unresolved domestic problems at home. Pastoral suicides reveal emotionally wounded and spiritually hurting people with an outward persona that had masked deep internal issues.

Discipling can do three things: (1) it can help a person deal with difficult matters in a safe and confidential environment, (2) it will point them to Jesus who is the healer of all matters, and (3) it can help equip them for effectively doing the work of ministry (Ephesians 4:11-12).

This brings us back to the purpose of this book. Discipling is critical to helping people solidify their relationship with Jesus Christ. As Christ is lifted up in a persons' life, they become positioned to receive the revelation that Jesus is the Christ, Son of the Living God.

What Happens When You KNOW Jesus is the Christ?

If you consider Paul's admonition in Romans 10:9-10, the first thing the new convert confesses is that Jesus is Lord, and that God has raised Him from the dead. Saying this is good, but knowing it is better.

And the Lord said, Simon, Simon, behold, Satan hath desired to have you, that he may sift you as wheat: But I have prayed for thee, that thy faith fail not: and when thou art converted, strengthen thy brethren. (Luke 22:31-32)

It was Peter (Simon) who declared that Jesus is the Christ, Son of the Living God. A few moments later, Jesus was rebuking satan in him (Matthew 16:16-23). He was the one disciple who walked briefly on the water, but also carried the distinction of denying Jesus three times in one night (Matthew 14:28-29; 26:69-75). In an act of reactionary protectionism, he sliced off the ear of one of those coming to arrest Jesus, and totally misread what took place on Mount Horeb (Matthew 17:4; John 18:10).

Then came the Day of Pentecost. One hundred and twenty people were filled with the Holy Ghost, and this same Peter who seemed so fearful and compulsive stood up and brought clarity to the events of that day (Acts 2:14). He was bold in his message to the curious crowd who had gathered. Something had clicked in his spirit. The Peter who had denied Jesus less than two months earlier, was now again proclaiming Him as Lord and Christ (Acts 2:36). This is the same change that anyone can experience. The revelation that Jesus is the Christ, Son of the Living God, prompted in us by the Holy Spirit, can cause us to do and say things that we previously were afraid to say or do.

Saul, who later became Paul, was a committed Pharisee, who brutally persecuted believers. On the road to Damascus he had a direct encounter with Jesus Christ. (Acts 9:3-6). This single encounter opened his eyes to the reality of the Lord. In an instant, he received the revelation that Jesus is truly the Christ, Son of the Living God (Galatians 1:15-16). Everything in his life changed from that day forward. At great personal loss and suffering, he boldly shifted into a mission to reach the Gentiles (Romans 11:13; 2Timothy 1:12).

He prayed for the believers in Ephesus that God would give them the 'spirit of wisdom and revelation in the knowledge of Jesus Christ'. He knew that once they received it, that they would never be the same (Ephesians 1:17-23). He insured that the believers in Corinth knew the Jesus who died, was buried and risen according to scripture (1Corinthians 15:1-6). He confirmed to Timothy that his capacity to endure great suffering was possible because he firmly knew who he believed (2Timothy 1:12).

Jesus called twelve young men to follow Him. During the approximately three years they were with Him, they constantly flip flopped and vacillated in their relationship. On several occasions they exhibited weakness and fear. Even after the Lord's resurrection, they had to be rebuked for their 'hardness of heart'.

And he saith unto them, Why are ye fearful, O ye of little faith? Then he arose, and rebuked the winds and the sea; and there was a great calm. (Matthew 8:26)

And he said unto them, Why are ye so fearful? how is it that ye have no faith? (Mark 4:40)

Afterward he appeared unto the eleven as they sat at meat, and upbraided them with their unbelief and hardness of heart, because they believed not them which had seen him after he was risen. (Mark 16:14)

When Jesus challenged their resolve to remain with Him, Peter reiterated his revelation from Caesarea Philippi in behalf of the whole group (John 6:69). They ran when Jesus was arrested.

One by one they gained glimpses of Jesus Christ, but it wasn't until Pentecost that they began to walk in the revelation of who He is. Their revelation was so profound that history records they died as martyrs for the Lord.

The Holy Spirit helps to remove natural, emotional and spiritual distractions from our lives. When they are removed, we can see Jesus, high and lifted up in authority over all things (Isaiah 6:1-4).

GOD DESIRES TO REVEAL HIS SON IN US

Several years ago, Gbile Akkanni, a Nigerian apostle, said that, "We don't serve a reluctant God." He went on to teach that God wants to do for us often beyond what we want Him to do. He is not holding back anything, but too often our expectations are so low that we limit what we receive.

Everything He does points us to Jesus Christ.

The written Word of God points to Jesus (John 1:1, 14; 2Corinthians 4:6; Revelation 19:13).

The Holy Spirit points us to Jesus Christ (John 15:26; 16:13-14).

Even creation is calibrated to help us receive divine revelation (Psalms 19:1; Romans 1:20). God wants to reveal His Son in us.

But when it pleased God, who separated me from my mother's womb, and called me by his grace, To reveal his Son in me, that I might preach him among the heathen; immediately I conferred not with flesh and blood: (Galatians 1:15-16)

I began this chapter by stating that most Christians have a cerebral knowledge of Jesus Christ. The Lord has been shown TO them through various bible studies, sermons, history and the like. These have their place, but they fall short of the greater point. Christ must be revealed IN us.

Paul was well educated. The great persecution he inflicted upon believers before his conversion suggests he knew about Jesus Christ. He had an intellectual understanding of Him and refuted Him based on His religious values (Galatians 1:13; 1Corinthians 15:9). His encounter with the Lord on the road to Damascus clarified to him that he was persecuting Jesus (Acts 9:5). This became the beginning point where he would shift from knowing about Jesus, to having Jesus being revealed in him.

Can we discover a pathway that will lead you to this revelation? I believe we can. Get ready to have Christ revealed in you.

9 | Becoming Positioned For Revelation

Peter's confession at Caesarea Philippi was a revelation directly from God. At the precise moment it was needed, he declared that Jesus was the Christ, Son of the Living God. Yet, within a few moments Jesus was rebuking satan who had used Peter to speak something totally against the will of God (Matthew 16:15-23). How did Peter go from being revelatory correct to being completely off base so quickly?

In this chapter I will address how we can position ourselves for divine revelation. Again, it must be reiterated that this book is not the source of divine revelation. It is however a roadmap that can help you align yourself with the Father so that He alone can speak fresh insights to you.

The fact that Jesus is the Christ, Son of the Living God is the primary revelation required for all believers in the ekklesia. It is upon this one single revelation that Jesus declared He would build. Any other revelations we receive are subject to this one.

HIGH THOUGHTS AND WAYS

For my thoughts are not your thoughts, neither are your ways my ways, saith the LORD. For as the heavens are higher than the earth, so are my ways higher than your ways, and my thoughts than your thoughts. (Isaiah 55:8-9)

Religion often pigeonholes itself into negative beliefs. This passage in Isaiah is often interpreted to suggest that we are incapable of fully understanding God. We resign ourselves to believing His high thoughts and ways leave us in a world where we rely on fate, rather than faith. "God is a mysterious God" or "You never know what God's gonna do", become escape clauses for failure to seek the Lord for answers in time of uncertainty.

Like many, I had read this section of Isaiah and assumed that all of God's ways were beyond my ability to comprehend them. I believed His thoughts were unknowable. This was an easy 'out-clause' whenever something happened in my life that I could not understand or explain. It was a study of Moses in a seemingly unrelated situation that helped me understand this matter.

SEEING THE FACE OF GOD

And Moses said unto the LORD, See, thou sayest unto me, Bring up this people: and thou hast not let me know whom thou wilt send with me. Yet thou hast said, I know thee by name, and thou hast also found grace in my sight. Now therefore, I *pray thee, <u>if I have found grace in thy sight, shew me now thy way</u>, that I may know thee, that I may find grace in thy sight: and consider that this nation is thy people. (Exodus 33:12-13)*

Moses sought the Lord for help in leading Israel. He specifically asked God *to show him His way*. This contradicted what I had been taught. I had believed that Moses had asked to see God's face. David wrote that God did in fact show Moses His ways, but Israel only saw His acts (Psalms 103:7). To be clear, Israel saw *what* God did, but Moses knew *why* God did it.

When Moses asked God to show him His way, it was more than getting a roadmap of the route to take through the wilderness. It was a request to understand God's purpose for the events surrounding their journey. As I read this account in Exodus, another seemingly contradictory matter arose. It was what appeared to be a contradiction that connected me with the passage we read earlier in Isaiah.

<u>And the LORD spake unto Moses face to face</u>, as a man speaketh unto his friend...(Exodus 33:11a)

Scripture clearly states that the Lord spoke to Moses face to face. This seems to be a direct contradiction of Exodus 33:20 that says no man can see God's face and live. How then could Moses talk with God face to face and survive?

With all humans, sight is precious. Yet, greater than sight is perception. It is how we interpret what we see that has the greater impact in our life. This explains why two people can literally see the same thing yet have entirely different responses. When we come face to face with our living God, our perception of His holiness has a tremendous effect on us. When we perceive how holy He is, the view we have of ourselves is immediately impacted. This is one reason that satan is tireless in his effort to distort our view of God. Your response to a mean, hard and vindictive God will be entirely different from seeing a loving and holy God.

For Isaiah, when Uzziah died his sight shifted from seeing a man he admired to the God he served. He considered himself ruined, and that he along with everyone around him was corrupt. He came to this conclusion because 'his eyes saw the Lord of Hosts' (Isaiah 6:5). The queen of Sheba had a similar reaction to Solomon. By no means am I suggesting that Solomon was God, but this incident reiterates how sight impacts us. After she saw the magnificent splendor and order in Solomon's house, there was 'no more spirit in her' (1Kings 10:5).

Think about Paul on the road to Damascus. The glory of the Lord was bright enough to literally knock him down (Acts 9:3-4; 22:6-7; 26:13-14). John on the island of Patmos saw the Lord and fell to the ground like a dead man (Revelation 1:17). Think about the fact that Jesus said the pure in heart shall see God (Matthew 5:8). Remember by following peace and holiness we position ourselves to see God (Hebrews 12:14). As sons, we get a view of Jesus that makes us as He is (1John 3:2). Whether you interpret all these as physical sighting or spiritual perception, the fact remains

116

that under certain circumstances we can see God. So, what does this have to do with God's high thoughts and ways?

God used these references relating to our sight or perception to help clarify not only how I saw Him, but how I understood Him. If I were to continue seeing Him as being way up and beyond my spiritual reach, and simultaneously see myself way down here struggling in the earth, then there would always be a gulf between us. By interpreting Isaiah 55 to mean God's ways and thoughts are so high above both my sight and understanding, I inadvertently resign myself to a distant relationship with Him. I would interpret God as being beyond my reach. I would see Him as remaining distant from me. But that was never God's intent. He wants to dwell among us and have us in His presence. He wants to commune with us.

> But as it is written, Eye hath not seen, nor ear heard, neither have entered into the heart of man, the things which God hath prepared for them that love him. BUT GOD HATH REVEALED THEM UNTO US BY HIS SPIRIT: for the Spirit searcheth all things, yea, the deep things of God. (1Corinthians 2:9-10)

Paul quoted a passage from Isaiah 64 specifically to address the matter of the source of the wisdom he had (1Corinthians 2:4-8). The natural eye could not see or perceive it, nor could the natural ear hear or understand it. Yet, it was readily available through the Holy Spirit for those who loved God. So when I reread Isaiah 55, this all began to make sense.

Yes, God's thoughts are higher than ours, and yes, His ways are higher than ours, but I realized that He made provision, even in the Old Testament to release His thoughts and ways to us.

For as the rain cometh down, and the snow from heaven, and returneth not thither, but watereth the earth, and maketh it bring forth and bud, that it may give seed to the sower, and bread to the eater: So shall my word be that goeth forth out of my mouth: it shall not return unto me void, but it shall accomplish that which I please, and it shall prosper in the thing whereto I sent it. (Isaiah 55:10-11)

The analogy of the rain and snow, and their impact on the earth show us God's intent to communicate with us. Rain and snow come down from heaven, and so does His Word. Both have specific purposes. The rain and snow are available to everyone who positions themselves to benefit from them. Likewise, the Word of the Lord is available to those who position themselves to receive from it.

The effect of the Word coming down and finding a place in our hearts has an immediate impact on us and our environment. We go out in the joy of the Lord. We are led by the peace of God. Everything around us will praise Him because we are properly aligned and walk in His revealed Word (Isaiah 55:12-13). Literally, all of creation is waiting for us to be in place (Romans 8:19). This becomes possible when we access Him through Jesus Christ (John 16:23).

To receive His high thoughts and ways, we must position our hearts to approach Him (Hebrews 4:12). The high thoughts and ways He shares with us become the revelation we need to navigate His purposes in the earth. In His presence is fullness of joy (Psalms 16:11).

When you come face to face with Him, expect to die. Expect to die to sin (2Corithians 4:10-11). Expect to die to ambition (Philippians 3:7). Expect to die to carnal wisdom (1Corinthians 4:4). Expect to die from your reliance on personal achievement (Romans 3:20; Ephesians 2:9).

In His presence expect to be exposed for who you really are. When you see yourself in the light of His glory, quickly repent so that He can extend you His mercy and speak His high thoughts and ways to you. (James 1:5-8, 17).

I pray that you see that God wants to reveal His thoughts and ways to you. However, our hearts must be pure to receive from Him. This brings us to another key fact, that we can be in position one minute, and completely out of sync the next.

THE MOMENT PETER WAS BLESSED

I wonder what Peter was thinking when He blurted out his now famous declaration of Jesus Christ identity. I wonder if He was aware that God was revealing to Him an eternal key for access into what the Lord would build in the earth. I would suggest that he was clueless. I came to this conclusion based on Jesus response to him.

> And Simon Peter answered and said, Thou art the Christ, the Son of the living God. And Jesus answered and said unto him, Blessed art thou, Simon Barjona: for flesh and blood hath not revealed it unto thee, but my Father which is in heaven. (Matthew 16:16-17)

Jesus said Peter was blessed because what he had said was a revelation that came directly from God. It is this 'blessing' that will help us to understand how we can receive revelation, too.

Be Blessed

The English word 'blessed' is one of those words that has been translated from multiple Greek words. The Greek verbs *eulogeo* and *eneulogeomai*; the adjective *eulogetos* and the noun *eulogia* suggests the act of speaking well of someone or something. However, there is another Greek word that Jesus used to describe how Peter was blessed – *makarios*. Jesus was not conferring a blessing on Peter. If that had been the case, the Greek word *eneulogeomai* would have most likely been used. Instead, He declared Peter as *makarios*.

Makarios is not a word that suggest you are conferring a blessing upon someone, but rather a word that indicates the emotional state of a person. Jesus used this form of being blessed several times in the Sermon on the Mount.

Blessed (*makarios*) are the poor in spirit...

Blessed (*makarios*) are they that mourn...

Blessed (*makarios*) are the meek...

Blessed (*makarios*) are they which do hunger and thirst after righteousness...

Blessed (*makarios*) are the merciful...

Blessed (*makarios*) are the pure in heart: for they shall see God...

Blessed (*makarios*) are the peacemakers...

Blessed (*makarios*) are they which are persecuted for righteousness' sake...

Blessed (*makarios*) are ye, when men shall revile you, and persecute you, and shall say all manner of evil against you falsely, for my sake. (Matthew 5:3-11 Abridged)

As you can see, every instance in this discourse, the Greek word Jesus used was *makarios*. The English word 'blessed' does not reveal the real concept of what is being expressed. In fact, there is not an equivalent English word that adequately expresses *makarios*. *Makarios* does not mean that a person is receiving a blessing, but rather that they are in a good emotional and spiritual place.

In their book, MISREADING SCRIPTURE WITH WESTERN EYES, E. Randolph Richards and Brandon J. O'Brien wrote:

The Greeks had a word for the feeling one has when one is happy: *makarios*. It is a feeling of contentment, when one knows one's place in the world and is satisfied with that place. If your life has been fortunate, you should feel *makarios*. We use idioms in English to try to approximate this experience. We'll say, "My life has really come together," or "I'm in a happy place," or "Life has been good to me." We are not really discussing the details of our life; we are trying to describe a feeling we have. *Happy* sounds trite, so we avoid it. Actually, we are *makarios*.[1]

Jesus revealed that the poor in spirit, who recognize their constant need for the Lord are *makarios*. They are in the right emotional and spiritual place. Mourning is brought to a place of comfort for those who are *makarios*. Every aspect of the Beatitudes begins with being *makarios*. It is the emotional and spiritual state of the individual that led to a specific outcome.

At Caesarea Philippi, Jesus said that Peter was *makarios*. I would suggest Jesus was saying that Peter was in a good emotional and spiritual place. It was in that moment that God revealed to him the eternal identity of Jesus Christ. Implicit is that we are more apt to hear from God when we are *makarios*. Frustration, fear, anger, discouragement, as well as pride, arrogance and high-mindedness block our ability to hear from God. In fact, all these carnal emotional and spiritual states open the door for the devil to influence what we think and say.

Jesus told his disciples that He was facing immanent death at the hands of the elders, scribes and chief priests in Jerusalem. Peter interrupted Jesus and said it would not be so. To this, Jesus immediately rebuked satan, as the source of what Peter had said. What happened to Peter being '*makarios*'? Jesus revealed that the

---

[1] MISREADING SCRIPTURE WITH WESTERN EYES: *Removing Cultural Blinders to Better Understand the Bible* © 2012 by E. Randolph Richards and Brandon J. O'Brien InterVarsity Press, Publisher Page 75

basis for Peter's off-course remarks was that '...his mind was not on the things of God, but on the things of men' (Matthew 16:23 Bible in Basic English). We are admonished by scripture to walk in the Spirit at all times (Galatians 5:16, 25).

The *makarios* place is our deliberate choice to remain in the presence of God. It is our intentional decision to be sensitive to the voice of the Lord, even when external circumstances threaten our comfort. It is to be confident that regardless of what we see, think or feel, God is working to do of His good pleasure (Philippians 2:13). It is in that *makarios* place that God can reveal His Son to us. How do you become *makarios*?

> *Giving thanks always for all things unto God and the Father in the name of our Lord Jesus Christ; (Ephesians 5:20)*

> *And whatsoever ye do in word or deed, do all in the name of the Lord Jesus, giving thanks to God and the Father by him. (Colossians 3:17)*

> *In every thing give thanks: for this is the will of God in Christ Jesus concerning you. (1Thessalonians 5:18)*

As you continue reading this book, be aware of your emotional and spiritual state of being. Consciously eliminate all worry and stress. You do this by being thankful in all things.

The pressures of life can be overwhelming at times, but by giving thanks in the midst of whatever you face you reduce the impact it has on you. I have found that when I give thanks, the Holy Spirit reveals what I need to navigate through any difficulty.

At times, He shows me my error that may have caused the problem. I can repent and position myself to be cleansed of my unrighteousness (1John 1:9).

There have also been times that the Holy Spirit will direct me to say or do something. Once I was thanking God for beginning to surround me with mature leaders. He instructed me to go to one of them and tell them that I wanted to ordain him as an elder. I was excited. But to my dismay, the person I approached responded angrily saying that I was arrogant to think I could ordain him. Needless to say, I was confused. I thought I had misunderstood God. Instead I learned a valuable lesson.

God knew what was lurking in that man's heart. He had ulterior motives for being in our ministry. He was waiting for an opportunity to take it over and push me out of the picture. The Lord knew what I didn't know. He knew what it would take to expose his true heart. I am convinced that the Holy Spirit, Who knew all things, directed me to approach him. Although it was painful, I had to thank God for protecting the ministry work He had entrusted to me.

I shared this to let you see that revelation is more than what we consider deep spiritual insights. The most common revelations you will receive are high thoughts and ways from the Throne of God to help you navigate through life. It all begins with the primary revelation that Jesus is the Christ, Son of the Living God.

10 | THE POWER IN THE NAME OF JESUS

Throughout this book, my emphasis has been to point you towards the single revelation that is vital to all believers; Jesus is the Christ, Son of the Living God. This must be more than a simple declaration. The revelation of Jesus Christ must become a deeply imbedded reality in your spirit that drives everything you do.

Knowing Jesus and *knowing about* Jesus are two different things. Atheist, agnostics, Buddhist, or Muslims can tell you about Jesus. They know about Him from their intellectual and historical understanding. But as believers, we must *know* Him. We must *know* Him beyond history and intellect. We must *know* Him as the Living Christ, Son of the Living God.

"Until now you have asked nothing in My name. Ask, and you will receive, that your joy may be full. (John 16:24)

In this chapter we will explore the power in the Name of Jesus. As you understand this, it can unlock the reality of our Living Lord in your spirit. When you realize and experience the power that is resident in His Name, your doubts and fears will dissipate. My prayer is that this chapter will stir you to see the undisputable power in the Name of Jesus.

THE DEVILS KNOW THE NAME...

Of course, it is believers who need the revelation of Jesus Christ. But we must realize the totality of His Lordship. He is not just Lord in the earth, but He is Lord in the heavens, the earth and everything beneath the earth (Philippians 2:9-10).

> Then some of the itinerant Jewish exorcists TOOK IT UPON THEMSELVES TO CALL THE NAME OF THE LORD JESUS over those who had evil spirits, saying, "We exorcise you by the Jesus whom Paul preaches." (Acts 19:13)

The sons of Sceva attempted to cast out a devil in the Name of Jesus that they only knew superficially. They only knew Jesus from what they had heard from Paul. They clearly had no personal revelation of Jesus Christ and it cost them dearly (Acts 19:13-20).

> And the evil spirit answered and said, "Jesus I know, and Paul I know; but who are you?" (Acts 19:15)

These itinerant exorcists knew *about* Jesus, but clearly they *did not know* Him. That fact was evident to the devils they encountered.

At a closer look, this incident reveals two critical things. First, it reveals that the Name of Jesus is more than the moniker of a man; it is the power of God resident in Him. Second, it reveals that whoever uses the Name of Jesus must have a personal revelation of who He is. Remember, the demons said that they knew Paul, as well as Jesus Christ. In other words, if Paul had cast them out, they knew they would have to go. Implicit in what the demons said is that they knew Paul had a revelation of Jesus Christ (Galatians 1:15-16).

The following passages reveal other incidents when the devils recognized the Lordship of Jesus Christ.

When He had come to the other side, to the country of the Gergesenes, there met Him two demon-possessed men, coming out of the tombs, exceedingly fierce, so that no one could pass that way. And suddenly they cried out, saying, "WHAT HAVE WE TO DO WITH YOU, JESUS, YOU SON OF GOD? Have You come here to torment us before the time?" (Matthew 8:28-29)

And the unclean spirits, whenever they saw Him, fell down before Him and cried out, saying, "YOU ARE THE SON OF GOD." (Mark 3:11)

Now in the synagogue there was a man who had a spirit of an unclean demon. And he cried out with a loud voice, saying, "Let us alone! What have we to do with You, Jesus of Nazareth? Did You come to destroy us? I KNOW WHO YOU ARE--THE HOLY ONE OF GOD!" But Jesus rebuked him, saying, "Be quiet, and come out of him!" And when the demon had thrown him in their midst, it came out of him and did not hurt him. Then they were all amazed and spoke among themselves, saying, "What a word this is! For with authority and power He commands the unclean spirits, and they come

127

out." And the report about Him went out into every place in the surrounding region. Now He arose from the synagogue and entered Simon's house. But Simon's wife's mother was sick with a high fever, and they made request of Him concerning her. So He stood over her and rebuked the fever, and it left her. And immediately she arose and served them. When the sun was setting, all those who had any that were sick with various diseases brought them to Him; and He laid His hands on every one of them and healed them. AND DEMONS ALSO CAME OUT OF MANY, CRYING OUT AND SAYING, "YOU ARE THE CHRIST, THE SON OF GOD!" And He, rebuking them, did not allow them to speak, FOR THEY KNEW THAT HE WAS THE CHRIST. (Luke 4:33-41)

In similar language from Caesarea Philippi, Jesus forbade the disciples from telling anyone that He is the Christ, Son of the Living God (Matthew 16:20). This was not an attempt to hide His identity, but rather to build on the idea that each of us must have the revelation of who He is.

The fact that the devils recognize the Lordship of Jesus Christ reveals the magnitude in His Name. It proves that anything you face, in any dimension, is under the Lordship of Jesus Christ and must bow to His authority. It further strengthens the need for you and me to have a solid revelation of Jesus Christ. It proves that everything in heaven, earth and beneath the earth must bow to the name.

EVERY KNEE MUST BOW TO THE NAME

Therefore God also has highly exalted Him and GIVEN HIM THE NAME WHICH IS ABOVE EVERY NAME, THAT AT THE NAME OF JESUS EVERY KNEE SHOULD BOW,

of those in heaven, and of those on earth, and of those under the earth, and that
every tongue should confess that Jesus Christ is Lord, to the glory of God the Fa-
ther. (Philippians 2:9-11)

In our classic western definition of the word *name*, we generally use it to identify a person, place or thing. But, in context of Jesus
Christ, the *name* is so much more than what identifies Him. It is
the essence of who He is in all the universe and it reveals everything the Father has deposited into Him.

Paul, in his letter to the Colossians makes a key statement
about Jesus Christ that finds some similarities in an Old Testament passage.

For in Him dwells all the fullness of the Godhead bodily; (Colossians 2:9)

"Behold, I send an Angel before you to keep you in the way and to bring you into
the place which I have prepared. "Beware of Him and obey His voice; do not pro-
voke Him, for He will not pardon your transgressions; FOR MY NAME IS IN HIM.
"But if you indeed obey His voice and do all that I speak, then I will be an enemy
to your enemies and an adversary to your adversaries. (Exodus 23:20-22)

It is important for us to see the correlation between these two
verses. For Paul to state that all the fulness of the Godhead was in
Jesus Christ implies that he had some basis for that belief. He may
have drawn his conclusions from what was recorded in the above
passage from Exodus.

As Israel was navigating its way through the wilderness, God gives Moses some interesting instructions regarding a unique Angel. This Angel would lead Israel in the way and ultimately bring them to the place that had been promised. Israel was instructed to obey Him, and not to provoke Him as He would not forgive their transgressions. This was specifically a result of God's Name being in this Angel.

Who was this Angel?

Theologians have long concluded that there were pre-incarnate appearances of Christ in the Old Testament. These are known as Christophanies. The fifth chapter of John has a remarkable progression of incidents that can help you understand this concept. I recommend that you read the entire chapter before reading the summary and highlights that follow.

SUMMARY OF JOHN 5

There was a man who had an infirmity for thirty-eight years. Jesus healed him and instructed him to take up his bed and walk. The Jews were angered because the man was carrying his bed on the Sabbath. When they discovered it was Jesus who healed the man, they sought to persecute Him because He had healed the lame man on the Sabbath (vss. 1-16).

But Jesus answered them, "My Father has been working until now, and I have been working." Therefore the Jews sought all the more to kill Him, because He not only broke the Sabbath, but also said that God was His Father, making Himself equal with God. (John 5:17-18)

What did Jesus do to anger the Jews? It was more than the fact that He had broken their limited view of the Sabbath, but also because He said God was His Father. By referring to God as His Father, the Jews understood that He had made Himself equal with God.

In response, Jesus outlined the relationship between Himself and the Father. He made clear the depth of the Father/Son connection. It was unmistakable. Jesus specifically said that, "those who fail to honor the Son, are in fact dishonoring God." He further said that, "the Son has the same life emanating from Him that the Father has." (vss. 19-26) He concluded that the Father "has given Him authority to execute judgment also, because He is the Son of Man" (vs. 27).

What Jesus said helps to connect Paul's statement to the Colossians with the Angel in Exodus. Jesus' assertion that He had authority from the Father parallels the authority given to the Angel in Exodus. When He declared that He has the same power emanating from Him that the Father has, this validates Paul's statement that "all the fulness of the Godhead was in Him bodily."

Earlier, I stated that our western understanding of the word *name* is what we call someone. However, we also use the word *name* to speak of a person's character and authority. For example, I could say that you have a good *name* among your peers. This would suggest that you are well respected. Or, you could be a representative of an agency. You would have the authority to act in behalf of that agency, or more precisely, you would function in the *name* of that agency.

In both the Old and New Testament, the words that are translated into English as *name* are similar in their definition. In the Old Testament, the Hebrew word *shem* implies the honor, character and authority of a person. In the New Testament, the Greek word *onoma* carries the same implication.

In Exodus 23:21, God said His Name was in the Angel. What does this mean? It meant that the honor, character and authority of the Father were in the Angel. It meant that God was in the Angel. As stated earlier, this may be why Paul wrote that 'all the fulness of the Godhead dwelt in Jesus Christ bodily' (Colossians 2:9). Again, this explains why this Angel had such broad perimeters.

Another hint that this was a Christophany, a pre-incarnate appearance of Christ, is the way God stressed how Israel was to obey Him.

> *"Beware of Him and obey His voice; do not provoke Him, FOR HE WILL NOT PARDON YOUR TRANSGRESSIONS...(Exodus 23:21)*

Israel had explicit instructions to obey the Angel. However, did you notice that the Angel did not have the authority to pardon

Israel's transgressions. On the surface that may seem to refute the idea that this was a pre-incarnate appearance of Christ. After all, didn't Jesus come to save sinners (1John 1:9)? That's the point. At the time Israel encountered this Angel, Jesus Christ had not gone to the cross to redeem mankind. They were under an entirely different covenant.

> *For this reason He is the Mediator and Negotiator of a NEW COVENANT [THAT IS, AN ENTIRELY NEW AGREEMENT UNITING GOD AND MAN], so that those who have been called [by God] may receive [the fulfillment of] the promised eternal inheritance, SINCE A DEATH HAS TAKEN PLACE [AS THE PAYMENT] WHICH REDEEMS THEM FROM THE SINS COMMITTED UNDER THE OBSOLETE FIRST COVENANT (Hebrews 9:15 Amplified Bible)*

At Calvary, Jesus redeemed us from the transgressions committed under the first covenant. In the wilderness, Israel was under that first covenant. The Angel, the pre-incarnate Christ, was leading them long before His redemptive work on the cross.

> *Let this mind be in you, which was also in Christ Jesus: Who, being in the form of God, thought it not robbery to be equal with God: But made himself of no reputation, and took upon him the form of a servant, and was made in the likeness of men: And being found in fashion as a man, he humbled himself, and became obedient unto death, even the death of the cross. WHEREFORE GOD ALSO HATH HIGHLY EXALTED HIM, AND GIVEN HIM A NAME WHICH IS ABOVE EVERY NAME: That at the name of Jesus every knee should bow, of things in heaven, and things*

in earth, and things under the earth; And that every tongue should confess that Jesus Christ is Lord, to the glory of God the Father. (Philippians 2:5-11)

It was on the cross that Jesus Christ exercised the ultimate act of obedience. He submitted Himself to the cruelest form of death in that era; the death on the cross. It was because of this that God exalted Him and gave Him a NAME above all names. The Name of Jesus would forever carry the same power of God throughout the universe.

I pray that you see that the revelation of Jesus Christ comes with the power in His Eternal Name. When you ask anything in the Name of Jesus, all the universe will align itself with the power in His Name. You speak with confidence because you know that all the fulness of the Godhead is in Jesus Christ, but also that you are complete in Him. This means that every principality and power must bow to the Name through you (Colossians 2:9-10).

As you meditate on the Name of Jesus, let me ask you one final question. What will it take for you to receive the revelation of Jesus Christ?

11 | WHAT WILL IT TAKE FOR YOU?

We are now at the place where the preverbal 'rubber hits the road'. It is the place where your actions today can impact the rest of your life. The revelation that Jesus is the Christ, Son of the Living God comes solely by the Holy Ghost. Yet, you must align yourself through the Word of God, repentance and prayer to receive it. If you desire the revelation of Jesus Christ beyond bible stories and religious tradition, the Holy Spirit is ready and willing to help you.

What will it take for you to truly get it? When will you have that epiphany, that 'aha' moment, that minute when the light comes on and you know, that you know, that you know you know that Jesus is truly the Christ, Son of the Living God?

Everything in my life's journey has been important to laying the foundation for me to really see Jesus as the Christ, Son of the Living God. The tipping point for me came through two specific chapters in a specific book. Everything I had studied in the Word of God, and much of what I had experienced, came together to unlock the revelation of Jesus Christ into my life.

The book I read was EVIDENCE THAT DEMANDS A VERDICT[1]. One of the chapters explored the life of Jesus Christ. Based on the claims He made about Himself, this chapter concluded He could only be one of three things: Lord, Liar or Lunatic. The other chapter dealt with the resurrection by asking if it was history or a hoax? That chapter alone eliminated all doubts I had regarding the bodily resurrection of Jesus Christ.

To be clear, I was already saved. I loved the Lord to the best of my ability. Yet, my faith in Him was limited to the denominational interpretation I had embraced.

I am thankful for the early days of my faith walk. There were principles imbedded in my spirit that continue to guide me today. The fact remains however, that no denominational system can replace the revelation of Jesus Christ as Son of the Living God.

As a maturing believer, I worked hard at living holy, yet I battled internal issues that I learned over time how to suppress. From time to time these deficiencies would come to the surface and I

---

[1] EVIDENCE THAT DEMANDS A VERDICT © 1972, 1979 Campus Crusade for Christ, Inc. Published by Here's Life Publishers, Inc.

would spend months battling my hidden disappointment, discouragement, and shame. At times it felt like I stayed saved by pure soulish grit and religious adrenaline. I developed an intellectual faith in Jesus. I could give you scripture and verse that described Him as our Savior, Lord, healer, and deliverer. I could say the right words, but I struggled to live the right life (Romans 7:15-25). Several of my acquaintances who were saved during that same time faced similar battles. Far too many of them backslid. Their inner conflicts and soulish desires overran the religious clichés.

Like many, I confessed that Jesus rose from the dead. Even so, my confession would often be challenged by my own thoughts. If I had tried to prove His resurrection, it would have been difficult for me. Praise God, the combination of the two chapters in EVIDENCE THAT DEMANDS A VERDICT brought Jesus to life in my spirit. I saw the reality of Jesus Christ more than I had ever seen before. My eyes were opened. My faith took a huge leap forward. The Jesus Christ of scripture became more alive than ever.

What has been the results? First, I really came to know that the Jesus of my proclamation was alive. He was no longer relegated to 'I believe it by faith' as my only defense against doubters. Now there is this deep inner knowing that Jesus is the Living Christ, Son of the Living God.

Second, my prayer life changed. I began to see that I was speaking to a trustworthy and living friend. Now, when I pray for others in His Name, I have the confidence that the Living Lord will be at work. Third, I no longer felt the need to 'prove' Him to others. Instead, I now present Him as a true and living friend. Fourth, when I face life's many challenges, I call on my Living Friend, Lord and Intercessor to help me.

For years I fought depression. During these episodes, days would pass when I did not speak to my wife or children. I hated the way I felt but was helpless to explain it. During that time, the revelation of Jesus being the Son of the Living God was growing in me. I am so thankful that the Living Jesus gave me strategy to overcome what I was dealing with. It has been well over thirty years and I have not dealt with depression.

During a particularly difficult time in our ministry, I was second guessing my every move. I often questioned my calling and direction. But the Living Jesus dispatched three angels to me to speak exactly what was necessary. They did not speak in generalities, they said exactly what I needed for encouragement and strength to persevere in the situation I was facing at that time.

There are many more testimonies I could share with you; from the unusual way He provided the home we live in today, to how He led us to the right place to save my wife's life. Today His presence is the norm in my life. I live with expectancy. Even as I write this book, I know I am writing about the Ever-Living Lord who is the Son of the Eternal God! But this book is not about me. It's for you. You may have testimonies that have blessed you over the years. They help to validate the presence of the Living Lord in your life. In fact, you may already have the revelation of Jesus being the Christ, Son of the Living God. But just in case there are any doubts lingering in you, I want to share a few last things that I pray will point you in the right direction.

Remember, the Holy Spirit reveals to us the Lordship of Jesus Christ (Matthew 16:17; 1Corinthians 12:3). The book I read only served as a catalyst to destroy religious barriers in my spirit. Through it, my unspoken doubts were eliminated.

Unspoken doubts are defined as areas of uncertainty in our own minds that wrestle with what we say. Before I read EVIDENCE THAT DEMANDS A VERDICT, I confessed that Jesus was alive. But inwardly, I felt inadequate to defend that confession. If someone had challenged me, specifically regarding the resurrection, I would have fallen woefully short. I had a historical understanding of Jesus. In conversations, I knew how to say the right things.

On February 13, 1974 I had a personal encounter with Him. That was my 'Damascus Road' experience. Immediately Jesus was presented to me in religious terminology. Believe me when I say I was being taught by solid, God loving people. They taught me what they knew and understood. But there were lingering questions that religious platitudes infused with scripture failed to address. These were my unspoken doubts. Thank God, the Holy Spirit knew me and provided me with the answers I needed.

This gets to the heart of this chapter.

For me, the Holy Spirit used the book EVIDENCE THAT DEMANDS A VERDICT. For you, He may use this book you are reading now that will align you to the reality of Jesus Christ. Yet, for others, He may use an event or a life changing experience to bring them to the full revelation of Jesus Christ. We cannot limit the ways the Holy Spirit may use. But rest assured, He is at work pointing believers to Jesus Christ (John 16:13-14).

What should you do? I encourage you to first and foremost be honest about any lingering doubts you may have. With the world constantly attacking and refuting the Word of God, at times it becomes difficult to know exactly what is or is not true. When denominational belief systems seem to contradict and battle each other, it becomes harder to know what to believe. Even as you read scripture, at times you may find it challenging to grasp what is being said. Nevertheless, God desires to reveal His Son to you in a deep and meaningful way. Therefore, being honest about your doubts gives the Holy Spirit an opportunity to reveal truth to you. No one can say that Jesus is Lord except by the Holy Spirit (1Corinthians 12:3).

It has been over two thousand years since Jesus literally walked on the earth. It is exciting to know that the same revelatory truth that was available to first century believers is available to us today.

Are You Too Familiar With Jesus?

Earlier in this book I shared factors that limit our ability to see Jesus; race, ideology, and culture. In this chapter, I want to add 'familiarity' as a serious hinderance to revelation.

> So all bore witness to Him, and marveled at the gracious words which proceeded out of His mouth. AND THEY SAID, "IS THIS NOT JOSEPH'S SON?" (Luke 4:22)

> AND THEY SAID, "IS NOT THIS JESUS, THE SON OF JOSEPH, whose father and mother we know? How is it then that He says, 'I have come down from heaven'?" (John 6:42)

Scripture reveals there were many people around Jesus when He walked the earth. They were physically with Him, but often they did not have the revelation of Him being the Son of the Living God. We assume that it would have been easier for those believers to really know Jesus. But often, they only saw 'the man' and were blinded by that limited view. They were so familiar with him that they could not really see Him. They knew His earthly father and mother, and as His ministry began to emerge, they could not see Him beyond what they knew about Him personally.

"IS THIS NOT THE CARPENTER, the Son of Mary, and brother of James, Joses, Judas, and Simon? And are not His sisters here with us?" And they were offended at Him. (Mark 6:3)

Mark wrote that familiarity caused some to be offended by Him. Jesus was amazed at their unbelief. As a result, His ability to do miracles among them was minimized (Mark 6:5-6).

Stop. Think about what you just read.

Miracles were limited because people were so familiar with Jesus that His ministry among them was hindered. Could it be that we are experiencing the same thing today? Why don't we see miracles, signs and wonders on a consistent basis? Have we become so familiar with the Jesus of our denominational rhetoric that we get offended when His truth crosses our religious boundaries? Is Jesus amazed at our unbelief, too?

What is familiarity? One of the definitions of familiarity is *the state of having knowledge about something. The expression 'familiarity breeds contempt' means that knowing a lot about someone or something can cause you to like that person or thing less.*

Familiarity can blind us to someone's potential. David was not considered among his older brothers who were presented to Samuel to potentially be anointed as king (1Samual 16:1-13). Joseph was looked down on by his brothers and misunderstood by his Father (Genesis 37:18-20). Familiarity will create incorrect assumptions. It will cause some to devalue a person. Familiarity is aligned with stereotypical conclusions that cause people to miss or ignore important details in others.

Notice what was familiar to the crowd around Jesus. They knew He was a carpenter. This was a noble profession, but one that did not particularly stand out among other types of work. No one in that day would consider a carpenter as the Son of God. The very thought of this would have seemed out of place. Today, most of us are familiar with what we have learned about Jesus. We know Jesus through a form of 'historical faith' similar to the way we believe historically about Abraham Lincoln, Thomas Edison, Martin Luther King, or Booker T. Washington.

Historically, we have learned that Jesus was a carpenter. Historically, we know that He was born in Bethlehem. Historically, we know He had brothers and sisters. Historically, we know He was crucified, and often we declare in a historical context that 'the bible says He rose from the dead'. Yet, these historical realities have often been diluted.

Religious traditions have reduced Jesus' birth to Christmas pageants. The crucifixion and resurrection are rehearsed once a year by Christians as a superficial acknowledgement of what took place at Calvary. Versions of the life, death and resurrection have been filtered through the lens of men who have used the facts around Jesus to fit a narrative that suits them.

This is not new. Paul wrote of those who preached their own variation of Jesus Christ (Philippians 1:15-18). The problem is two-fold. First, these variations hamper the ability to see Jesus as He is. Second, these variations become engrained and accepted as doctrinal truth. These versions of truth become so familiar to its followers that other versions of Jesus seem in error. This is what I want to alert you to in this chapter.

> *When Jesus came into the region of Caesarea Philippi, He asked His disciples, saying, "Who do men say that I, the Son of Man, am?" So they said, "Some say John the Baptist, some Elijah, and others Jeremiah or one of the prophets." He said to them, "But who do you say that I am?" Simon Peter answered and said, "You are the Christ, the Son of the living God." (Matthew 16:13-16)*

In response to the Lord's first question, it is obvious that there were several interpretations relating to His identity. When Jesus asked the disciples who they thought He was, Peter's declaration did not tie the Lord's identity to any human – dead or alive. He declared Jesus as the Christ, Son of the Living God. Jesus Christ. The Son of Man was not the reincarnation of dead prophets. Jesus Christ, the Son of Man came as a man but was the Son of the Living, not dead God (Luke 20:38; Psalms 2:7; Hebrews 1:4-5).

The list of prophets first mentioned were admirable and well known by the people of Jesus day. There was a level of familiarity that most people had. They would place Jesus in good religious company. However, each of these prophets fell short of the Lord's identity. Shortly after their experience at Caesarea Philippi, Jesus took Peter, James and John up a mountain where He was transfigured before them. It was there that God declared for the second time, "This is my beloved Son in whom I am well pleased". Then He added, "Hear Him" (Matthew 3:17; 17:5).

If you were to ask people today who Jesus is, I imagine you would receive a variety of answers. But this query must be directed toward you. Who do you say Jesus is? Do you have the indwelling revelation that Jesus is the Christ, Son of the Living God? Don't fear your answer, instead be honest about it. If you sense any, I repeat, any amount of doubt in your response, you have a foundation from which to build. See your doubts as a revealing of issues that hinder how you see the Lord.

THREE THINGS TO CONSIDER

No human can give you the revelation of Jesus being the Christ, Son of the Living God. It is even difficult to explain what that revelation feels like. It would be like me trying to explain what it feels like to have my father as my father, my mother as my mother or even my wife as my wife. I can give you emotional expressions, but whether you believe it or not, I know what I know regarding my relationship with them all. There is nothing anyone can say that will diminish this reality.

Likewise, my relationship with my Living Lord is the same. I can't prove it to you, even though I may be able to express it through personal testimonies. But you may or may not believe my testimony (although I pray you do). The reality is that the Holy

Spirit will reveal Jesus Christ to you in such a manner that His reality becomes incontrovertible in your spirit.

Peter wrote that we should 'grow in grace and in the knowledge of our Lord Jesus Christ' (2Peter 3:18). Paul's desire was to know Him in the power of His resurrection (Philippians 3:10). I am confident that you are reading this book because you want to know Jesus in the deepest and most intimate way. My prayer is for you to come to that revelatory place (Ephesians 1:17-20).

The following are three things you can do daily.

1. ## Ask God to reveal His Son to you

   I believe God desires to reveal His Son to you. We do not serve a reluctant Creator. The bible declares He has given us all things that pertain to life and godliness (2Peter 1:3). It was at Caesarea Philippi that Jesus declared that He would build His ekklesia upon believers having the revelation of who He is – the Christ, Son of the Living God (Matthew 16:16-18). Why then would the Father withhold the deepest revelation of His Son from anyone? Jesus told His disciples not to tell anyone that He is the Christ. Why? Because anyone who follows our Lord must have a sure knowing of exactly who He is (2Peter 1:12). Daily, ask for a greater revelation of the Lordship of Jesus Christ.

2. ## Practice His Prescence

   Be bold in obedience. Sometimes we don't know what the outcome will be of our actions. Don't allow the unknown to restrict your obedience. Regarding God's Word, I heard it said that comprehension is not a prerequisite to obedience. You practice the presence of our Lord by stepping out in faith and doing what you know to do. You make every move in the Kingdom as if Jesus is physically there with you. If the Word declares to 'lay hands on the sick and they will recover', then lay hands on the sick. Once you do, the rest is up to the Lord. Peter and John encountered a man who was lame from birth. They took him by the right hand and instantly he was made whole. When they were questioned about how this happened, their answer was simple, "...that it is by the Name of Jesus Christ of Nazareth, whom you crucified and whom God raised from the dead—it is, I say, by his Name that this man stands here before you lame no longer" (Acts 4.10). Practice His presence by doing what you know to do in His Word and trusting Him to do the rest.

3. <u>Don't Dilute The Word</u>

God's Word is a lamp unto our feet and a light unto our path (Psalms 119:105). We must treasure it and abide by it. There is a foolish teaching growing in some Christian circles that the bible is no longer necessary or relevant.

I strongly disagree. Without the Word of God, we have no guide to follow (Psalms 119:133). Without the Word of God, our spirit remains unclean (John 15:3; 17:17).

It has always been the ploy of the devil to distort the Word of God. From the beginning satan was at work twisting and diluting scripture to the point of ineffectiveness. Doctrines of devil's breed confusion in the religious world (1Timothy 4:1). As you seek the revelation of Jesus Christ, learn to read the scripture for what it says, and not what somebody said it says. Above all, seek the direction of the Holy Spirit to reveal God's Word to you. Don't forget, Jesus is the Word of God (John 1:1; 1:14; Revelation 19:13). Trust Him to open the scriptures to you (Luke 24:27, 45).

Of course, be steadfast and prayerful in your pursuit of our Lord. I believe that you can be among the millions of believers being raised up in this season to bring the influence of the Kingdom into the earth. Get ready!

12 | JESUS CHRIST SON OF THE LIVING GOD

I believe with every fiber of my being that Jesus is the Christ, Son of the Living God. Every chapter in this book has been to point you to that one reality – that one revelation – that one truth that commands the attention of the Kingdom of Heaven. This chapter is no exception. Prayerfully, a foundation has been laid in you for the Holy Spirit to reveal Christ to you in a deeper and more meaningful way.

There are dozens of scriptural references that point to the reality of Jesus identity. Many have been inserted throughout this book. Without question, some passages will be repeated in this chapter. Even so, what you are about to read is necessary to crystalize what scripture says about His Lordship. There must be a combination of the Word of God and the Holy Spirit to position you to receive and walk in the one revelation that supersedes all others. We are beckoned to a greater place by them both.

Each weekday morning, I teach a short message on Facebook Live known as Good Morning, Ekklesia. Each episode is a Study Starter with the purpose of provoking deeper study in subjects relating to ekklesia.

Ekklesia has been mistranslated and misunderstood for centuries. Yet, it is the ekklesia that Jesus said He would build with those who have the revelation that He is the Christ, Son of the Living God. Failure to grasp the necessity of this revelation serves only to perpetuate the status quo, leaving countless believers reliant upon religious rhetoric and presuppositions to live by. Jesus is the Christ, Son of the Living God. You must do all you can to align yourself with this powerful and primary revelation.

This is my challenge to you in this final chapter. I have organized a few key scriptures topically and added some commentary to help you think more about the revelation that Jesus is the Christ. Get with other believers and pray through what you read. Trust the Holy Spirit to show you our Lord

DEMONIC CHALLENGE TO JESUS' IDENTITY

Matthew 4:3 And when the tempter came to him, he said, If thou be the Son of God, command that these stones be made bread.

Matthew 4:6 And saith unto him, If thou be the Son of God, cast thyself down: for it is written, He shall give his angels charge concerning thee: and in [their] hands they shall bear thee up, lest at any time thou dash thy foot against a stone.

Immediately after being baptized by John the Baptist, the heavens opened and a voice spoke from heaven saying, "This is my beloved Son, in whom I am well pleased (Matthew 3:17). This was a voice of confirmation. This voice left no ambiguity as to who Jesus is – the beloved Son of God. But who was this voice speaking to? Who at that moment needed to know that Jesus was God's beloved Son?

John knew Jesus as the Son of God by the sign of the Spirit descending upon Him (John 1:32-34). There is no biblical evidence that John heard the voice from heaven. So who heard the voice? I would suggest that only Jesus and the devil heard it.

Immediately after being baptized, the Spirit led Jesus into the wilderness to be tempted of the devil (Matthew 4:1; Mark 1:12; Luke 4:1). It is the nature of that temptation that you need to understand. The devil's complete motive was to bring Jesus' identity as the Son of God into question. Twice he challenged Jesus with, "If you are the Son...". In other words, the devil was attempting to make Jesus second guess the last thing He had heard prior to going into the wilderness. In a third attempt, he offered Jesus the Kingdoms of this world. That too was a veiled attempt to subvert His sonship. Jesus knew that at the time appointed by the Father, that the Kingdoms of this world would become His (Revelation 11:15).

The fact that the devil would bring into question Jesus identity as the Son of God reveals the magnitude of this truth. The devil would never address something that did not pose an imminent threat to him. If Jesus had questioned His own identity, it would have been devastating to you and me. Thank God, Jesus knew who He was, and you and I can be victorious today because we know that He is the Christ, Son of the Living God.

Demonic Recognition of Jesus Christ

Matthew 8:29 And, behold, they cried out, saying, What have we to do with thee, Jesus, thou Son of God? art thou come hither to torment us before the time?

Mark 3:11 And unclean spirits, when they saw him, fell down before him, and cried, saying, Thou art the Son of God.

Mark 5:7 And cried with a loud voice, and said, What have I to do with thee, Jesus, [thou] Son of the most high God? I adjure thee by God, that thou torment me not.

Luke 4:41 And devils also came out of many, crying out, and saying, Thou art Christ the Son of God. And he rebuking [them] suffered them not to speak: for they knew that he was Christ.

Luke 8:28 When he saw Jesus, he cried out, and fell down before him, and with a loud voice said, What have I to do with thee, Jesus, [thou] Son of God most high? I beseech thee, torment me not.

Scripture teaches us that every knee will bow to the Name of Jesus Christ. This includes things in heaven, in earth, and beneath the earth. In other words, there is no dimension of existence that will not one day bow to the Name of Jesus.

Several times throughout Jesus' earthly ministry, demons recognized Jesus. They knew His authority, and they knew they had to submit. This adds to the incontrovertible reality that Jesus is the Son of God.

ANGELIC DECLARATION OF CHRIST IDENTITY

Luke 1:35 And the angel answered and said unto her, The Holy Ghost shall come upon thee, and the power of the Highest shall overshadow thee: therefore also that holy thing which shall be born of thee shall be called the Son of God.

Before Jesus was conceived by the Holy Ghost, He was already identified as the Son of God.

HUMAN CHALLENGES TO JESUS IDENTITY

Matthew 27:39-42 And they that passed by reviled him, wagging their heads, And saying, Thou that destroyest the temple, and buildest it in three days, save thyself. If thou be the Son of God, come down from the cross. Likewise also the chief priests mocking him, with the scribes and elders, said, He saved others; himself he cannot save. If he be the King of Israel, let him now come down from the cross, and we will believe him.

In the passage above, there were by-standers and religious leaders who mocked Jesus on the premise of Him being the Son of God.

This reveals that those who mocked Jesus had no clue of who He really was. Their perception of Him being the Son of God was twisted and confused. Their literal view of the destruction and rebuilding of the temple revealed they did not understand He was referring to His body (John 2:19-21). Religious systems try to justify themselves by what they perceive to be your failures.

INDIVIDUAL RECOGNITION OF JESUS' IDENTITY

Matthew 14:33 Then they that were in the ship came and worshipped him, saying, Of a truth thou art the Son of God.

Matthew 16:16 And Simon Peter answered and said, Thou art the Christ, the Son of the living God.

Mark 15:39 And when the centurion, which stood over against him, saw that he so cried out, and gave up the ghost, he said, Truly this man was the Son of God.

John 1:34 And I saw, and bare record that this is the Son of God.

John 1:49 Nathanael answered and saith unto him, Rabbi, thou art the Son of God; thou art the King of Israel.

John 6:69 And we believe and are sure that thou art that Christ, the Son of the living God.

John 9:35 ¶ Jesus heard that they had cast him out; and when he had found him, he said unto him, Dost thou believe on the Son of God?

John 11:27 She saith unto him, Yea, Lord: I believe that thou art the Christ, the Son of God, which should come into the world.

Acts 7:56 And said, Behold, I see the heavens opened, and the Son of man standing on the right hand of God.

Acts 8:37 And Philip said, If thou believest with all thine heart, thou mayest. And he answered and said, I believe that Jesus Christ is the Son of God.

Acts 9:20 And straightway he preached Christ in the synagogues, that he is the Son of God.

Romans 1:3-4 Concerning his Son Jesus Christ our Lord, which was made of the seed of David according to the flesh; And declared to be the Son of God with power, according to the spirit of holiness, by the resurrection from the dead:

2Corinthians 1:19 For the Son of God, Jesus Christ, who was preached among you by us, [even] by me and Silvanus and Timotheus, was not yea and nay, but in him was yea.

In chapter eleven, I shared how the Holy Spirit used specific chapters in a specific book to bring me into the revelation of Jesus Christ as the Son of God. The passages above reflect the testimony of several believers who appear to have received that powerful revelation. Beginning with Peter, then the centurion, John, Nathaniel, the blind man, Stephen, the eunuch baptized by Philipp, and of course Paul, each of these individuals appear to have received the revelation of Jesus Christ being the Son of the Living God.

Can you add your name to the list? This book cannot give you this revelation. Only the Holy Spirit can do that. You can be assured that He is willing and waiting to reveal Christ to you.

VICTORY PROMISED FOR KNOWING JESUS IDENTITY

What have we learned? We have learned that when we receive and walk in the revelation of Jesus Christ as the Son of God, that we have gained access to the power and authority of the Kingdom of Heaven. We have learned that all the resources of the Kingdom of Heaven will be provided to us. We have learned that we are authorized to legislate Kingdom policies in the earth through binding and loosing. Above all, we know that we can move with confidence knowing that in His Name all things are possible.

When Peter declared the Jesus is the Christ, Son of the Living God, Jesus immediately said that it would be on that revelation alone that He would build His ekklesia. Jesus first declaration made our victory sure. He said that those who have the revelation that He is the Christ, Son of the Living God can move forward knowing that the gates of Hades cannot prevail against them. Let that sink into your spirit. We begin from a platform of victory.

I encourage you to meditate on the following passages, and recognize that the revelation of Jesus Christ being the Son of God guarantees your victory.

> Hebrews 4:14 Seeing then that we have a great high priest, that is passed into the heavens, Jesus the Son of God, let us hold fast [our] profession.

Don't waver in your victorious profession. In this passage, profession is translated from the Greek word *homologia*. It means to acknowledge. We should never waver in our acknowledgment that we have a great high priest in the heavens, Jesus the Son of God.

> 1John 4:15 Whosoever shall confess that Jesus is the Son of God, God dwelleth in him, and he in God.

Let it come out of your mouth. Confess that Jesus is the Son of God until it is deeply engrained in your spirit. Confess it when you have doubts. Confess it amid adversity. Confess it when everyone else is denying Him. Confess it when you have to stand alone. God promises to dwell in you, and you will have the comfort in knowing you dwell in God.

> 1John 3:8 He that committeth sin is of the devil; for the devil sinneth from the beginning. For this purpose the Son of God was manifested, that he might destroy the works of the devil.

From this point forward, stay focused on the reality that Jesus, the Son of God came to destroy the works of the devil. He utterly decimated satan and the underworld on the cross (Colossians 2:14-15). Our victory is forever settled in the heavens.

> 1John 5:5 Who is he that overcometh the world, but he that believeth that Jesus is the Son of God?

The ekklesia is built with overcomers. Everyone of them who have been called out believes that Jesus is the Son of God. Imagine a dynamic Body of Believers who overcome anything the world throws at them. Believe and overcome.

> 1John 5:9-13 If we receive the witness of men, the witness of God is greater: for this is the witness of God which he hath testified of his Son. He that believeth on the Son of God hath the witness in himself: he that believeth not God hath made him a liar; because he believeth not the record that God gave of his Son. And this is the record, that God hath given to us eternal life, and this life is in his Son. He that hath the Son hath life; and he that hath not the Son of God hath not life. These things have I written unto you that believe on the name of the Son of God; that ye may know that ye have eternal life, and that ye may believe on the name of the Son of God.

> 1John 5:20 And we know that the Son of God is come, and hath given us an understanding, that we may know him that is true, and we are in him that is true, [even] in his Son Jesus Christ. This is the true God, and eternal life.

What is eternal life? It is more than living forever. Jesus said that eternal life is to know God and the one he has sent (John 17:1-3). Now is the time to walk in eternal life. Now is the time to know God and the one He has sent, Jesus Christ, His Son. This is where I close this book. I ask you to seek Jesus as the Christ, Son of the Living God. You may already be saved, but don't shy away from assuring your heart before Him (1John 3:19-24).

I end this book where it began; at Caesarea Philippi. The challenge is to you. Look around you. The world needs the glorious power of the Kingdom of Heaven. You can authorize in earth what the Kingdom of Heaven has authorized. You can bind in the earth what has been bound in the Kingdom of Heaven. You can move forward confidently knowing that the Gates of Hades cannot defeat you. You can be well equipped by utilizing the keys of the Kingdom of Heaven. But it requires one thing to activate you into this dimension of living. It's the one thing that has been the focus of this book. The power you have to literally change your world begins when you receive the primary revelation needed by every believer, that 'Jesus is the Christ, Son of the Living God!'

Father, I pray that You will reveal Your Son to the person who has read this book. I pray that You will empower them to fulfill every assignment You have entrusted to them. I pray that the God of our Lord Jesus Christ, the Father of glory, may give to them the spirit of wisdom and revelation in the knowledge of Him. Father open the eyes of their understanding that they may know what the hope of His calling is, as well as the riches of the glory of His inheritance in them. Above all, give them revelation by which you will build your ekklesia, that Jesus is the Christ, Son of the Living God. In Jesus' Name! Amen!

OTHER BOOKS BY TIM KURTZ

LEAVING CHURCH BECOMING EKKLESIA
Because Jesus never said He would build a church

THE BELIEVERS GUIDE FOR LEAVING CHURCH BECOMING EKKLESIA

7 FACTS WHY JESUS DIDN'T SAY HE WOULD BUILD A CHURCH
...and what it means to you

NO LONGER CHURCH AS USUAL
Restoring First Century Values and Structure to the 21st Century Church

For more information visit *www.TheEkklesiaCenter.org*

My desire in this book has been to peel away many obstacles that can keep you from the revelation of Jesus Christ as the Son of the Living God. Cultural barriers are internalized impediments that can obscure your view. These barriers are often unnoticed. Early in the formulation of this book, I reached out to Dr. Leonard Robinson to provide input pertaining the culture of the Kingdom. The more you recognize the depth of the kingdom culture, the more likely you are to recognize the Lord of the Kingdom. Dr. Robinson's contribution can be found on page 82. His brief biography and contact information is below.

Blessings,

Tim Kurtz

DR. LEONARD ROBINSON is an Apostle and Founder of Kingdom Vision Ministries International located in Philadelphia, PA -USA.

He is an author, public speaker, mentor, business coach and an entrepreneur. His primary message is the Kingdom of God. He also teaches the nuances of business formulation, development of ideas and what it takes to launch a business emotionally.

Dr. Robinson hosted REBUILDING THE BLACK FAMILY CONFERENCES with Dr. Myles Munroe, Psalmist Archie Dennis and others. He also hosted THE KINGDOM CULTURE BIBLE CONFERENCES from 2008-2014 with Dr. Myles Munroe, Dr. Cindy Trimm and Dr. Kelly Varner.

Dr. Robinson is the founder of several companies. As Managing Partner of Omega Marketing Services, LLC., he brings innovative payment solutions to the finance sector of government and businesses in Africa, the Caribbean and other parts of the world.

He serves on the Board of Directors of Accelerated School of Christian Ministries International (ASCMI) -USA and Ukraine. In 2009 he received an Honorary Doctorate for his extensive studies on the Kingdom of God. His work was ultimately presented as curriculum Universities in Uganda and Malaysia. He regularly meets with leaders of state government in Africa as well various business leaders in Manila and Hong Kong.

Dr. Robinson has ministered to over 155,000 people through his broadcast, conferences, workshops, seminars and email. You can contact him at:

Dr. Leonard Robinson
Kingdom Vision Ministries International
P.O. Box 24532
Philadelphia, PA 19120
Website: www.drlenrobinson.com